MANAGING FOR INNOVATION

MANAGING FOR INNOVATION

The Mindmix Guide to Organisational Creativity

Neville I. Smith, BA, FAIM
and
Murray Ainsworth, BSc (Hons), MBA

MERCURY BOOKS
Published by W.H. Allen & Co. Plc

First published in 1989
by the Mercury Books Division of
W.H. Allen & Co. Plc
Sekforde House, 175–9 St John Street,
London EC1V 4LL

ISBN 1 85251 061 7

Set in Meridien by Phoenix Photosetting, Chatham
Printed and bound in Great Britain by
Mackays of Chatham PLC, Chatham, Kent

FOREWORD

The layout in this book may be different from other management books. We think this is appropriate, as the book deals with innovation and new ideas. It should be novel. For example, you'll see that each chapter is subtitled as a M-I-X. Why? Quite simply, the topic of innovation in organisations is about mixing things . . .

- mixing analytical and intuitive processes
- mixing convergent and divergent thought
- mixing people to make productive groups

and, more specifically, mixing the potentials of two different brains. And here we take a liberty and use 'mind' instead. Thus, *Mindmix*.

Mindmix is not a theory. It is a practical base for managing towards innovation that we have used in many organisations and with hundreds of groups and it works. We hope you find it useful, rewarding – and enjoyable.

NEVILLE SMITH
MURRAY AINSWORTH

CONTENTS

Part 3: Mindmix Application

Part 1

MINDMIX

Background and Innovation

1
CREATIVITY AND INNOVATION IN ORGANISATIONS:
An Introduction to Mindmix

Managing Innovative Xcellence

There was an old tramp sitting on the park bench, enjoying the sun. I sat next to him.

'Hello,' said I.
'Hello,' said he.
'Nice day?' said I.
'Nice day,' said he.
'Enjoying the sun?' I asked.
'No, I'm busy. I'm thinking,' he answered.
'Sorry,' said I, 'I didn't mean to interrupt.'
'That's okay . . . I've worked hard enough today. I've plenty of new thoughts.'
'Really? What'll you do with them now?'
'They're not important. They're only ideas about making park benches more comfortable. I'm an expert at something . . . it's either park benches, or thinking about them. I'm not sure which.'
'I guess you're probably expert at both. But I'm interested . . . how could you make this bench more comfortable?'

'Well, I've plenty of ideas for that.'

'Why don't you tell the city council?'

'Oh, they don't want my ideas. They've got an engineer. He knows all about the benches. I saw him here one day measuring them up. Of course, he doesn't sit on them.'

'Did you talk to him?'

'Started to, but he told me not to be ridiculous and laughed. So I put my ideas back in my head. They're safer there.'

How similar to this are things in your organisation? Have you got a few thinkers who aren't listened to? Perhaps you're one yourself at least some of the time? Do your people sometimes feel like the tramp? Is it possible you're sometimes the city engineer? And have you got plenty of good park-bench measurers?

As consultants we work in many organisations trying to help them find novel answers to business problems, and trying to stimulate creativity. We know there are plenty of good ideas which stay in the safest place (the head). We know the park bench isn't only in the park. There are park benches and park-bench measurers in every organisation in the land. There are also tramps – wasted idea-talent – in many organisations.

Without exception the top management of the organisations with which we work would claim to be looking for or encouraging creativity or innovation. And almost without exception we have discovered powerful negative forces at work which make it difficult for new ideas to surface. Without new ideas, there's no innovation. Through this work in organisations and some related research we have evolved methods of minimising these negative forces and increasing the chances of new ideas emerging and surviving. So we've put pen to paper, to describe 'How?' as fully qualified tramps.

If you're an occasional tramp sitting on an organisational park bench with a head full of unexpressed ideas, this book can help you get your ideas out of the safe place (the head), both for yourself and your fellow park-bench regulars. If you're a park-bench measurer, this book can show you how to acknowledge the ideas of the park-bench regulars, without chasing their potentially great ideas back into their heads. And if you're the city council, worried both about your park-bench measurers and your tramps, this book is for you too. It can show you processes to get the two talking and working together, and to come up with a new park bench that suits both of them and keeps your bank manager (who's probably a park-bench measurer) happy.

The question of encouraging creativity and innovation in organisations is not a light one. It's not a matter of novelty for novelty's sake, nor is it merely a little light relief. Sound adaptive and developmental processes lead to increased productivity and growth. At best failure to innovate means repeating yesterday tomorrow. At worst it means sharing the fate of the dinosaurs: they lost the ability to adapt; they failed to respond to changes in their world. They're extinct. An important difference between them and you is that, although they didn't have the power to change things, to respond in novel and different ways, to innovate for survival and growth, you do! And that's the big collective 'you' – it includes you the person, and the organisation or group with which you are involved.

You *can* innovate; you can get new ideas. There is a substantial body of research about the how and why of creativity and innovation, and many proven, effective, practical techniques for making innovation happen. This book's objectives are to present this knowledge in down-to-earth language, and to supply relevant practical techniques. It is, to a considerable degree, a 'how to' book, deliberately written to help you understand the concepts and use the techniques.

Being innovative and creative is not difficult. It's as easy as waking up. And it's just as necessary as waking up.

Innovate: What's the alternative?

There's no doubt that this tail-end of the twentieth century has been, and will continue to be, dynamic. 'The only constant is change' is a well-worn phrase. Perhaps it needs updating: 'the only constant about change is that it is constantly accelerating'. Change moves upon each of us like waves on a beach; you can ignore the first wave or two, but the tide is coming in, and you have to move, to adapt, to seek a new dry place. At least you *can* move away from the waves (and at least you can be confident that the tide will turn). The quality of your responses, the combination of ingenuity and excellence, is what will differentiate you from your competitors, from the also-rans, and from the extinct dinosaurs . . . they were caught in the waves.

A manager's role has always included a concern for the future, and for adaptive responses to it, but not all innovation is merely adaptation. Innovation can also obviously be predictive, ahead of change. It can cause change. Some would argue that this is why change is increasingly upon us. The argument goes that we used to have needs-driven technological improvements, but that now we have technology-driven change. Studies of innovation show that both market-pull and technology-push innovations abound. We don't really want to get into that argument here: our objectives are more specific. We're talking about any sort of innovation, as long as it's relevant to you. Both responsive and predictive ingenuity are of interest, and the tools discussed in this book are applicable to both. They are also applicable to any size organisation: the same tools apply whether you belong to a five-person charity organisation or a multinational conglomerate employing thousands. We've used them at all levels, with success. So can you.

What is 'innovation'?

One reason people get involved in esoteric arguments about innovation is a general preoccupation with definition. Both laymen and academics spend a great deal of time making fine distinctions, which often are of little practical value. For

THE INNOVATION PROCESS – PEOPLE

It may help to think of the innovation process as one which involves several different kinds of people. Sometimes, several kinds may reside in the same individual. That's not uncommon in small business, but less common in large.

- **The creative person** has ideas. These are his or her output.
- **The innovator** translates ideas into reality. Action leading to tangible products or services is the output.
  (**The inventor** may be a composite of 1 and 2.)
- **The entrepreneur** is the person who by business ability develops the product or service into a moneymaking proposition. Final outcome is product or service success.
- **The intrapreneur** is a person who pursues entrepreneurial-type innovation, but within the framework of a large organisation.
- **The 'champion'** is one who picks up an idea, not necessarily his or her own, and through tenacity, belief and commitment works it through the organisation to a successful outcome.
- **The 'sponsor'** is usually a senior manager who believes in the idea and the team, and quietly clears the way, by influencing key people, for the idea to pass through various stages of organisational scrutiny.

example, key words here are 'creativity', 'invention', 'innovation' and 'entrepreneurship' (and, more recently, 'intrapreneurship'). We could spend this entire chapter on definitions but we're not going to. There wouldn't be enough space and, secondly, you'd probably stop reading. And if we sometimes use 'creativity' and 'innovation' as virtually synonyms, we apologise now. Forgive us our sins, for we have committed them with our eyes open.

In the broadest sense innovation includes the idea of invention and discovery, but goes beyond it. It is anything that provides usable, unique novel solutions to problems, opportunities or challenges – whether small or large. Some examples might be a new use for an old product; a new product from on-the-shelf technology; a novel marketing strategy; novel organisational structures for new activities; new designs of machine or man-machine systems to increase productivity; recognition of new market segments; development of new (hopefully simpler) internal systems; faster ways to gather, process and disseminate information, etc. They can be simple or complex. We are not concentrating only on the big break-throughs in this book. Our work has shown us time and time again that many little changes and adaptations can sometimes be more significant than one apparently major breakthrough. But we're not ignoring the big ones either.

Why Mindmix?

A quick answer might be: 'To avoid half-wits'. One of the scientific breakthroughs of the past ten years has been an expanded understanding of how the human brain works. The brain is now known to have two distinct parts, virtually halves, doing distinct things. It's as if each person has two brains: one for analytical thought, the other for more holistic, intuitive thinking. Of course, if any one person were to spend all his or her time using only one half of the brain, we could with some justification call him or her a 'half-wit'. Perhaps the long-gone creators of this term knew more about the brain than they let on? And perhaps you know some of these 'half-wits', people who think only analytically, or people who think only intuitively?

Now we know that for creative or innovative thought to occur, and for ideas and associations to be recognised and put into practice, the whole brain is needed. That is **Mindmix, the process of using *both* halves of the brain together (but not necessarily simultaneously).**

We also know that some people are more analytical than others while others show intuitive strengths. These qualities can be recognised, and there are group processes which allow us to capitalise on these different strengths. It's like making one supra-whole brain out of two or more available brains which have complementary differences. This is also Mindmix.

We're not saying managers need to be neurologists or psychologists: in fact, managers who play pseudo-psychologist usually cause more problems than they solve. We will concentrate on the tools and techniques you can use as a manager to capitalise on the brain as we know it.

Our knowledge of the brain shows that within any group of people there is an enormous, virtually untouched, innovative resource. Many of our well-established social and managerial practices are known to work against fully using this resource (and these will be discussed in Chapters 3 and 4). And many of these practices are easily varied. Not to do so would be an irresponsible waste of this enormous resource. **Practical advice as to how to realise the full potential of your brain, and the brains of your employees, is a major thrust of this book.**

'Invention is the Mother of Need'

Caught us, eh? Shouldn't it be: 'Need is the mother of invention'? Well, we don't care. Sure there's invention that is virtually demanded by need, but there's also invention that stimulates need. We said earlier we wouldn't debate the difference between technology-driven change, and need-driven technology change. Both are alive and well. This is the same point, so we won't argue it. But we reintroduce it to stress *ideas*. All innovation, all invention, all creativity, starts with ideas.

There are always ideas. We've all suffered from 'mental constipation' on occasions; a flow of ideas sometimes just won't come. But we all know this is a temporary phenomenon; relief from 'mental constipation' always seems to come. If you have difficulty coming up with an idea, someone else who may know very little about your problem may offer an unusual but useful answer, or a 'laxative'.

INVENTIVE TRIVIA

It is not unusual to find the kernel of a great idea in the minds and words of someone ignorant of the specialist field. Perhaps they don't know enough to know it can't be done!

- The **diving bell** was invented by an **astronomer** (Edmund Halley).
- The **pneumatic tyre** was invented by a **veterinarian** (John Dunlop).
- The **safety razor** was invented by a **salesman** (King Camp Gillette).
- The **seed-drill** was invented by a **lawyer** (Jethro Tull).
- The **cotton gin** was invented by an unemployed **law graduate** (Eli Whitney).
- The **modern vacuum** cleaner was invented by a **bridge-builder** (Hubert Booth).
- The **hydraulic jack** was invented by a **cabinet-maker** (Joseph Bramah).
- The first practical **submarine** was invented by an Irish **school-master** in New York.
- The **hydrofoil** was first thought of by a French **priest** – and the **knitting frame** by an English **vicar**.

More recently, the inventor of an electronic 'scarecrow' which repels flying-foxes from fruit trees got the idea from seeing a doctor carry out an abdominal scan on his pregnant wife.

You don't have to be 'expert'!

Why is this so? We will look at specific answers later, but it's important to note here that idea sources are frequently in-expert; often their relevance to the problem in hand is hard to see. This may be the 'bumblebee syndrome': the bumblebee doesn't know he can't fly; he has never studied aerodynamics, yet he flies! Or it may be that we're all poor judges of others' intellects; we judge by years of schooling, social polish or smooth talk.

Whatever the reason, as a manager you need to know both the 'why' of idea sources, and the 'how' of getting ideas. We'll cover this very fully in Part 2. (Check above: here's some evidence of the odd sources of ideas, at least developed ones.)

A Closer Look at 'the Problem'

Some people view problems as closed-ended, while others recognise them as open-ended. Closed-ended problems are those which require a specific answer, the 'correct' one. Open-ended questions are those which a great multitude of alternative answers may satisfy. In business, we often mistakingly see our open-ended problems as closed-ended. Someone else, with a different perspective, may well see our old chestnut from a fresh perspective and, by nothing more than the recognition of its open-ended nature, be able to supply us with a idea.

One of the most important uses for creative 'tools', or methods, in in checking, right at the outset, that you are working on the right problem. Clever solutions to the wrong problems are of little value. While this sounds obvious, our world is full of solutions to non-problems. The supersonic Concorde may be one of them. The rotary automobile engine for family vehicles is quite possibly another: it certainly hasn't achieved the dominant position projected for it in the 1970s. Look back over your organisation's track record on launching new products or new services. Some of those you'd rather not dwell on may have been solutions to the wrong problem.

Looking at the problem area from different perspectives will often get you closer to the essence of what needs to be resolved. For the over-stressed manager, is 'the problem' . . .

- How to reduce stress levels at work?
- How to learn to manage existing stress levels more successfully?
- How to use leisure time more effectively, to compensate better?
- Or how to find a less stressed position elsewhere at the same level of reward?

Maybe, of course, it's a mixture of all of these – or at least of the first three. But defining the problem precisely with a clear statement of what needs to be worked on is usually a necessary first step in the search for solutions.

Our bias is towards open-ended problems. Not all management questions are open-ended, but often problems are inappropriately defined in a closed-ended manner. We're better educated at such tight thinking than at loose thinking, so we close things down. We look for neat analyses. We drift into agreement with colleagues about the nature of a particular problem. So take the time to clarify a problem or issue. Simply writing it down so that it can be communicated to others (that is, clarified) can save you hours, months or even years of effort. Much of what is covered in Chapter 6 as 'redefinitional techniques' can be used to help you clarify problems and establish unambiguous starting points.

Implementing Ideas

If Mindmix stopped at the stimulation and generation of ideas, it would not offer much to you. You will learn techniques with the potential for several million recorded ideas in a few minutes. No, we're not joking; you'll learn at least one technique with that potential. And it's been proven – over and over again. But getting ideas at that rate causes a special problem of selection. Which one of millions is 'best' is difficult to assess.

Every bit as important as generating ideas is screening and evaluating these ideas. The process of idea survival and innovation is Darwinian; not all ideas and inventions deserve to survive. Idea screening and evaluation in some form take place in all organisations. In the excessively bureaucratic organisation, not only the survival of ideas but the emergence of ideas is constrained by successive layers of 'approval'. People believe they have a right to see, hear and comment on any new idea. It's an 'it-impacts-on-my-area' syndrome that not only scares off the idea generators, but also raises a sort of competition to see who can find the smallest, or most ridiculous, reason to kill

So you like definitions? Try these . . . and add a few . . .

Creativity is having another go.
Creativity is turning down a sideroad.
Creativity is looking again.
Creativity is climbing out of your box.
Creativity is daring to differ.
Creativity is throwing sand in the wind.
Creativity is not saying that's impossible.
Creativity is solving the impossible.
Creativity is using both halves of your brain.
Creativity is trusting daydreams.
Creativity is doubting the doubters.
Creativity is having a pack of 53 cards.
Creativity is frequent failure, occasional wins.
Creativity is

?

Some more definitions. Add some yourself . . .

Innovation is doing it differently.
Innovation is finding a better way.
Innovation is a 350 km/hour train.
Innovation is a light which switches itself on.
Innovation is a talking car.
Innovation is

an idea. In less bureaucratic organisations the odds on idea survival may be slightly better, but sorting the good from the less good remains a critical task.

Similarly, all organisations have some means of planning the implementation of new things. But new ideas are often born ugly and ultra-sensitive. At the outset, a new idea is often not sufficiently well formed to withstand the heavy scrutiny more appropriate to refined proposals. More than anything, the idea may need development rather than immediate evaluation. It needs special polishing to turn ugly to smooth, and special handling to prevent damage. And not all gross planning methods, those suitable for the 'new' marketing plan which is in effect last year's with the numbers changed, are sufficiently probing and detailed to handle the truly new.

This book is structured in three parts. Part 1 concentrates on introducing the basic innovation (and Mindmix) concepts. In Chapters 3 and 4 the book explores the implications of innovative processes for managers and organisations. Chapter 5 tackles the subject of innovation in strategic planning. Too often, strategic processes are based on, or even tend to be, statistical projections, or lead only to carefully worded documents. The need for innovative strategies should be self-evident.

In Part 2, we concentrate on tools and techniques . . . first, those related to getting new ideas (Chapters 6 and 7), and secondly those related to screening, evaluating and caring for these new ideas. But we stress here: this is not a book on systematic decision-making (Chapter 8). That's a well established series of processes already much written about elsewhere. But we do stress the opportunities for synergy (Mindmix) presented by these processes.

In Part 3 (Chapter 9), we offer guidance for your use of the concepts and tools covered by Mindmix for your organisation. You are encouraged to try to apply the concepts and tools within your own organisation. Additional reading is also suggested.

This book thus progresses from necessary knowledge,

through available techniques, to application. So far we've only stressed the need for innovative intent, and outlined what we'll be covering in each of the other interactive elements in the book.

You are now entering the world of Mindmix. We wish you a pleasant, and useful, trip.

2
Your Two Brains

```
Mental Inner Xcitement
```

A psychologist named J.P. Guildford coined the phrases 'divergent' and 'convergent' in the early 1950s to describe different thinking styles. He, as had many others before him, observed that people seem to think in two distinct ways; simply, any one individual tends to be dominantly either a convergent thinker or a divergent thinker.

Convergent thinking is the sort of thinking most of us are trained to do – that is, in order to find the answer to a problem we look for a logical train of ideas that are linked in an ordered way so that we can find the one 'correct' answer. Convergent thinkers seem most prepared to work in a rational, systematic way, with an orderly arrangement of information. Convergent thinking is particularly valuable for closed-ended questions, where there is usually one 'best' answer, with the answer based on logic, such as if $x = 2$ and $y = 8$, what is $3x + y/2$? Or how much interest will be payable on my bank account in the last quarter?

Divergent thinking is quite different from convergent thinking. It is a sort of intuitive thinking useful to deal with problems permitting several possible solutions, where novel, unexpected answers have potentially equal acceptability with more readily observed answers. It is useful with problems where there is no one right answer, like: 'How could we make Libya the tourist capital of the World?' or 'What will we call our new product?

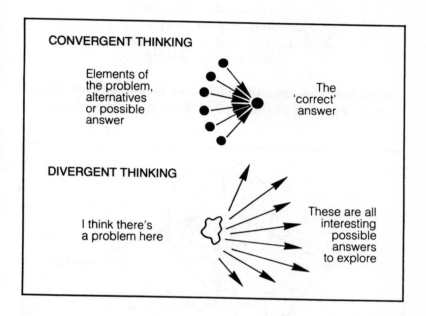

Divergent and convergent thinking are contrasted in the figure above.

Now, this is not quite a black-or-white issue. Each of us is capable of both divergent and convergent thinking. But we're not all equally capable, and nor do we show the same preference for these two types of thinking. Some are more prepared to enter into divergent thinking than others; still others seem to be happier if more consistently involved with convergent processes.

This convergence/divergence split is one of the many dichotomies noted in descriptions of human behaviour. People are seen to be:

logical or intuitive
objective or subjective
intellectual or emotional
realistic or imaginative
planned or impulsive
discriminative or integrative
directed/structured or 'free-wheeling'
quantitative or qualitative

Why so many two-part divisions? And they're not new observations; reporting of this type of dichotomy is as old as the

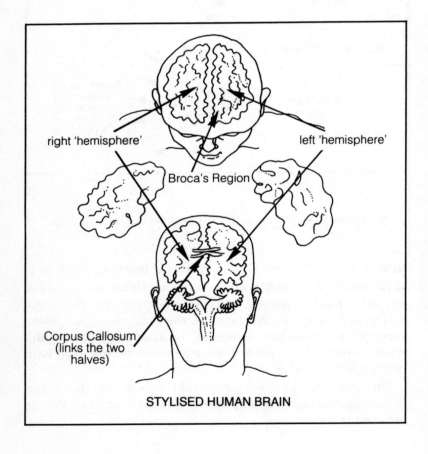

right 'hemisphere'

left 'hemisphere'

Broca's Region

Corpus Callosum
(links the two
halves)

STYLISED HUMAN BRAIN

Chinese Yin and Yang. The answer may be revealed by recent research which shows that each of us does, in fact, have two distinct thinking parts of our brain.

Physiologically, our brain has two distinct hemispheres: one on the left side, and one on the right. The diagram on page 26 illustrates this.

We now know these two halves do totally different jobs. The function of the left side of the brain is linear thought, the type of thinking involved when you are solving a mathematical problem or writing a formal report. The right side of the brain acts or behaves in a different way; its functions are connected with imagery, such as recognising one face from among many, and with intuition or 'gut-feel'. The table on page below outlines the known differences in the hemispherical functions.

Left brain	Right brain
Linear/sequential (A-B-C-D-E---)	Non-linear 'flashes' of insight (A-M-C-F-B---)
Rational/analytical	Intuitive/'gut feelings'/Holistic
Verbal (somewhat 'language bound')	Non-verbal/visual-spatial
Deductive	Inductive ('experiential')
Quantitative	Qualitative

Special note: Language skills are controlled by a small area called Broca's Region, or the 'language lump', usually located in the left hemisphere. In some people, this is reversed. For more detail on hemispherical specialisation and associated phenomena, such as 'left-handedness', the interested reader should refer to the Further Reading section at the back of the book. While it would be easy to expand this section, as it has many interesting areas of research and many side-routes of some relevance, we do not consider this to be the major topic or purpose of this chapter nor of the book. Viewing the brain as a black-and-white split may not be useful, and is certainly inaccurate.

There is an obvious parallel between convergence/divergence and the left brain/right brain model. Simplistically speaking, convergent thinking takes place in the left brain. Divergent thinking occurs in the right brain, although some creative thought may involve the entire brain. It's not the exact geography that's important. What matters is that we can see a relationship between the important convergent/divergent concept and the physiological structure of the brain. This two-part brain model may offer similar explanation for many of the language dichotomies listed previously. Certainly, there are important observations of significance for managers involved with generating new ideas and innovation in general.

Hemispherical Dominance

Duality and lack of symmetry seem to be part of being human. At the gross level, everyone is 'handed', 'footed' and 'eyed' to one side or the other. Every man who shaves is aware of his asymmetry; perhaps one ear is lower than the other, or his beard is fuller on one side than the other. Every woman who applies make-up sees similar minor differences. We're all somewhat lop-sided; we've one foot marginally bigger than the other, or a shoulder lower than its partner, or whatever.

Most specifically, we have two separate brain hemispheres, and they're not necessarily equal. Anatomical difference between hemispheres has even been measured in foetuses; we're apparently born with a particular bent one way or the other.

The preference for activity in one hemisphere or other of the brain is called hemispherical dominance.

As Professor Henry Mintzberg has pointed out, a person may be smart and dull at the same time.[1] An artist may have great difficulty in expressing himself in words, while an accountant may be essentially incompetent as a painter. Both are 'smart' in things which involve their dominant hemisphere. This is not only true of the artist and the accountant, it's true for each of us.

And there are clearly pressures in our society which would make us believe that 'convergent smart' is the preferable mode.

Pressures towards Convergence

In our culture it would appear that for most the left brain is dominant. Whether the majority of us are born with a left-brain dominance, or whether we develop towards being convergent thinkers as a result of the educational and socialisation processes, are questions the researchers have yet to answer. But even though anatomical differences in the hemispheres are known to exist in the youngest of babies, there are certainly pressures that affect our thinking styles as we grow. These may hide our right-brain tendencies, and that's a great pity; the right brain is the home of our potential for divergent thinking and so is the source of many innovative ideas.

There seems little doubt that our educational system is pre-occupied with left brain activities. The 'three R's' is still the basic message in education; 'if you can't read, 'rite, or do 'rithmetic, how will you survive?' Of course, other subjects such as art and music are more or less intruded into the curriculum, but for many children these are extras or luxuries. Every school pupil knows not to reveal too much imagination in his or her essays; the risk of casual ridicule (probably not intended as such by the teacher) is too great. And every university student knows how to ensure a pass: 'give them what they want!'

The pressures towards convergent, left-brain thinking are not limited to school. The divergent thinker who unwittingly offers his oddest idea to a group of 'friends' quickly learns the power of ridicule. He or she is less eager to state an opinion next time around! And the nine-year-old kid who offers strange-sounding advice to the truck-driver unloading a heavy load is quickly told his advice is not needed (at least, that's what the driver probably means by his colourful expletives).

Analytical, left-brain skills are in great demand. To be known as 'highly analytical' is generally accepted as a compliment. Of course, to be known as 'a little odd' is not generally accepted as a compliment. And yet the truly divergent person may be somewhat different. Even modern technological advances, which should provide an opportunity for man to be deliberately divergent as increasingly complex machinery handles convergent tasks, seem to have increased the demand for linear, rational skills. Can you imagine what would happen if your computer programmer or systems analyst suddenly shot off at a tangent?

Despite these pressures there *are* people who are 'right-brained', who prefer to work on open-ended problems via divergent processes. There are others, probably but not necessarily the majority, who can be called 'left-brained', and who prefer to work on closed-ended problems via convergent processes.

Creative people are not necessarily high achievers at school.

Observations of individuals in seven US colleges who had been identified as behaving creatively indicated that between 50 and 80 per cent of these individuals dropped out of school before graduation. This was significantly higher than the drop out rate among the rest of the student body.

Think what this may mean for the location of creative people in your organisation. There's clearly a better statistical chance that they are low in the organisation.

(Reitz, H.J., *Behaviour in Organisations*, Irwin, 1981)

Divergence, and Right-brain Dominance

Extremely 'right-brained' or divergent individuals are rare. In our Western societies, we tend to condone the extreme without fully embracing them. They typically drop out of school early, and may be judgementally (and not necessarily accurately) labelled as 'unintelligent' and 'slow learners'. They are at an obvious disadvantage in the educational system; if you can't give 'right' answers, you're obviously 'wrong'. They are similarly at a disadvantage for employment opportunities; who wants to hire an oddity?

But every manager should wonder seriously what might be lost by hiring only the 'look rights', only the strongly convergent thinkers. Rejecting the drop-out, the potentially truly divergent individual, is fairly common practice – but is it a valuable practice?

Of course, we all have some divergent ability, and we all have a right brain. And some good divergent thinkers clearly learn to play the convergent game and end up in good positions inside organisations. But this is trusting to luck.

Recently, we were talking to a personnel manager of a large organisation. He was describing his difficulty of finding people who would 'fit into our culture'. We suggested that it might be better to find someone who would 'rock the boat' a little. He wouldn't see the reasoning. Yet he was working in what could best be described as a mediocre organisation. Certainly, it had a safe, secure culture. And continuing to hire towards that culture has, to us, obvious end-results. 'Rocking the boat' isn't necessarily wrong. It may be a way of introducing desirable divergence.

Let's digress, and consider the case of Albert Einstein. For many, the image will be of the scientist, the great mathematician surrounded by his formulae and figures, the ultimate rational, left-brain thinker. Yet Einstein dropped out of school at fifteen, with poor grades and no diploma. And his ideas came as pictures and images; he only later put them into words and mathematical symbols to communicate to others.

It is reported that one summer's day Einstein was lying on a hillside contemplating the rays of light shining into his half-closed eyes. He was dreaming of what it would be like to travel down a light beam – when he had a sudden insight, an intuitive 'right-brain' image of what it would be like. And so the Theory of Relativity was born. We can't, of course, be certain that Einstein was a 'right-brainer', but his ideas were certainly divergent for his day. And imagery of the type reported above is commonly reported by many other outstanding scientists and great inventors.

Of course, accepting divergent people is not as easy as it sounds; they're not all budding Einsteins. Without them, however, the chances of finding the truly novel solutions are reduced, for only someone capable of giving the totally different answer can give it – and that's the divergent thinker!

The most novel idea may, by its very nature, sound the most ridiculous. In an age when lighting was provided by oil lamps and candles, a person wanting to 'light a fire without a flame in a vacuum in a sealed bottle' must have sounded very strange indeed. But that's a perfectly adequate description for an electric light bulb. (The filament was, incidentally, demonstrated by Joseph Swan in Britain in 1878 almost a year before Thomas Edison's more dramatic demonstration in the USA.)

Divergent thinkers commonly express their ideas in a clumsy manner; the ideas are 'rough' at birth. In many cases, this could

---

RIGHT-BRAIN IMAGERY

'Words or language do not seem to play any role in my mechanism of thought. The physical entities which seem to serve as elements in thought are certain signs and more or less clear images.'

Albert Einstein (*Scientist*)

'I saw in a dream a table where all the elements fell into place as required. Awakening I immediately wrote it down on a piece of paper. Only in one place did a correction later seem necessary.'

Dmitry Mendeleev
(*creator of the periodic table of elements*)

Sources: Ghiselin, B. (ed.), *The Creative Process*, Berkeley, University of California Press, 1952; Krippner, S.,' 'The Creative Person and Non-ordinary Reality', in *Gifted Child Quarterly*, 1972 (16), pp. 203–28.

be because the idea is from the right brain. It's a generalised image or concept that the individual must translate into words so as to communicate with others.

The 'roughness' of new ideas adds another opportunity for ridicule. This has serious implications for managers (discussed in Chapter 3). But despite roughness, despite oddity, it is the activity of the right brain, and the intuitive, gut-feel responses to problems which you must respect if you are to manage for new ideas and innovation. The right brain may not be the only source of new ideas, but it is a valuable source of novelty.

Creativity and the Whole Brain

In management development activities associated with idea and innovation management, we commonly divide the innovative process into three major elements. These we call idea-generation, idea-evaluation, and idea improvement/

RELATIONSHIP BETWEEN INNOVATION AND RIGHT/LEFT BRAIN

Innovation element	Comment	Cerebral activity
Idea-generation	Sorting out problem areas, and listing alternative ideas, including the novel ideas	Right brain, divergent thinking is essential
Idea-evaluation	Screening some from many, and detailed evaluation of the some	Left brain, convergent thinking is required for analysis
Idea protection/ improvement	Improving the 'rough' idea, and determining strategies for its development and improvement	Whole brain, both divergent and convergent thinking are required

protection. The relationship of these to left-brain/right-brain processes is set out on page 33. Idea evaluation is primarily a combination of screening and decision making. It is a vital process for management, as switched-on right brains and encouraged divergence can generate very large numbers of ideas.

Different elements of the innovative process require different styles of thinking, and call upon either hemisphere of the brain. Creativity is thus not the exclusive property of the right brain. It's a whole brain process. But getting full access to the right brain is critical if totally novel ideas are to be found.

Accessing the right brain, and generally stimulating divergent thinking, may be new to many managers. But it's not difficult, as you'll see in Part 2 of this book. And it's also not enough for innovation. Yes, it's necessary if you are to find truly novel answers. But you also need to evaluate, improve and protect new ideas to be ready to implement them. And that means you're involved with whole-brain processes, that is,

---

A RIGHT-BRAIN 'FLASH'

A report by the Dutch chemist Kekulé, who was attempting to synthesise benzene:

'I turned my chair to the fire and dozed. Again the atoms were gambolling before my eyes. The smaller groups kept modestly in the background. My mental eye, rendered more acute by visions of this kind, could now distinguish larger structures, of manifold conformations, long rows sometimes more closely fitted together, all twining and twisting in snake-like motion. But look! What was that? One of the snakes had seized hold of its own tail and the form whirled mockingly before my eyes. As if by flash of lightning I awoke.'

As a result, Kekulé was able to write down the now famous formula for the benzene ring. This report appears to illustrate two features of right-brain thinking: visual imagery, and sudden intuitive insight.

(Koestler, A., *The Act of Creation*, Macmillan, 1969)

with both hemispheres, and with people of both divergent and convergent strengths. You're involved with Mindmix.

Measuring 'Right-brainedness'

Researchers into the brain have established refined measures to determine hemispherical specialisation and dominance. These include electroencephalographs (EEG's), thermodynamic measures of energy consumption (activity), use of CAT scanners and other elaborate techniques. These are essential for such research, but are not readily available for management situations. And you might well add, 'fortunately'. In management, mapping the geography of right and left brains is not as important as finding the clues to convergence and divergence which will pay handsome dividends. We need to learn to recognise the different strengths of individuals for group synergy (that is, Mindmix), and to put individuals of different dominance together into problem-solving teams.

For many years psychologists have experimented with tests of divergence and/or creativity. A great many of these were devised before hemispherical dominance was understood. These tests try to measure creativity, not right-brainedness. In practice, the more traditional tests tend to predict achievement in areas such as creative writing rather than in, say, business management. More recently, tests designed specifically to measure hemispherical dominance have been developed. Four well known ones are the Alert Scale of Cognitive Style[2], the Hermann Brain Dominance Instrument[3], a test called Your Style of Learning and Thinking[4], and the Mobius Psi-Q1 test[5]. The Alert Scale of Cognitive Style uses 21 questions in a forced-choice format. Physiological variation is difficult to measure accurately even with modern physical science instruments so it is hard to see how such a short questionnaire could give an accurate measure. The Hermann Brain Dominance Instrument is longer, possibly overcoming to some degree the criticism of the Alert Scale, but its author makes some very unequivocal claims about its accuracy as a measure of hemispherical dominance and professional reaction to these claims is divided. The major external validation studies for the Hermann Brain Dominance Instrument have been against EEG measures, but EEG measures are not universally accepted as an accurate measure of dominance. The third test, Your Style of Learning and Thinking, may have more to offer. Its developers have a substantial history of involvement with creativity testing. The Mobius Psi-Q1 test measures the management style (left brain, right brain, or integrative) that executives claim to actually use in their on-the-job decision making. It has been fairly widely used in the USA.

In our practical work, we use none of these measures. Instead, we use a device called 'Decision Preference Analysis' (DPA, for short) which has been generally commercially available for managers' use since 1983. DPA has been established as highly valid in measuring quantitative versus qualitative cerebral preferences. The authors of this device, Drs. J. Kable and R. Hicks[6], make no direct claims for the device as a measure of brain dominance, although we are aware, from personal discussions, that a limited series of EEG correlations have been conducted, and that these correlations have been surprisingly

---

ENCOURAGING RIGHT-BRAIN ACTIVITY

One prominent inventor known to us works between midnight and 4.00 am in his home laboratory because, he says, 'it is the perfect time to create and invent'.

It's interesting to note that normal intrusions, which are language (left-brain) based, would be eliminated by this practice. This person's nocturnal habits are his way of encouraging right-brain activity.

Another inventor, a very successful graphic designer, goes home to do his creative thinking – usually before dinner, but often in the shower before breakfast. Showering is a non-language-dependent, tactile (right-brain based) activity.

A DIFFERENT VIEW OF THE RIGHT BRAIN

In some languages, 'left' and 'right' have peculiar connotations. In English 'right' can mean 'correct'. In French *droit* can also mean 'straight, not perverse'. In Italian 'destro' signifies the right hand, but can sometimes mean 'clever'. By contrast, *sinistro* comes from the Latin 'sinister', meaning 'left'. Other cultural and language plays on 'left' and 'right' abound. Some have been listed by Russell in his *The Brain Book* and the following table shows part of these summary associations (but note that the 'right hand' is the 'left brain'):

Right (left brain)	Left (right brain)
male	female
west	east
good	evil
pure	impure
joy	sorrow
health	sickness
heaven	hell
sun	moon
day	night
yang	yin
active	passive

(Russel, P., *The Brain Book*, Routledge & Kegan Paul, London, 1980)

high. The warning about EEG data is still valid here, but the DPA has other solid validity data. Of course, the correlations are not too surprising; quantitative and qualitative preferences are apparently descriptive of subsets of right-brainedness and left-brainedness.

We find DPA provides an extremely useful guide in our work. The score is produced simply as a quantitative (QN) versus qualitative (QL) percentage split. A high QN score is, say, 75:25 (QN:QL). Predictably an individual with this pattern will behave in a rational, sequential manner in a decision-making situation. A high QL score is, say, 25:75 (QN:QL). An individual with this pattern will behave in an intuitive, 'gut-feel', and idea-generative way in a decision-making situation. Most of us come somewhere between these two extremes, with the average very close to 50:50.

We have had many opportunities to observe different QN:QL patterns in group decision-making situations. In management development workshops to do with creative decision-making, we commonly split the group into a highly quantitative sub-group, a highly qualitative sub-group and a '50-50' sub-group. Each sub-group is given the same task, to complete a criteria list for a marketing decision to a time limit. Typically, the highly quantitative sub-group completes a very precise set of criteria, carefully laid-out and weighted, finishing close to the time limit. The '50-50' sub-group completes a useful list, but not with the detail of the quantitative sub-group, and tends to finish a little early (and usually discusses ways to satisfy the criteria). The highly qualitative group is still discussing at the end of the time, and has a list of possible actions but *no* criteria. Its members always use the time to generate alternative actions and ideas despite clear instruction to set criteria. In short, the highly qualitative sub-group displays what one would expect from a group of right-brain-dominant individuals, the highly quantitative group displays what one would expect from a group of left-brain-dominant individuals, and the '50-50' group displays a little of each.

This exercise is very revealing to participants. It is interesting that in subsequent decision-making exercises the individuals readily admit to each others', and their own, weaknesses and strengths, and readily accept some leadership behaviours of the '50-50'. The '50-50's' are seen to understand both sides of the argument.

The brain is a wonderful organ; it starts working the moment you get up in the morning and does not stop until you get to the office.
Robert Frost (1874–1963) quoted in Byrne, R.,
The 637 Best Things anybody ever said, Sphere Books, 1984.

DPA is not as yet validated as a test of right- or left-brain dominance, and in its present form may never be. But it certainly is a test of quantitative versus qualitative cerebral preference. As we've said before, the geography is probably unimportant in practical management. Although the cerebral preference pattern is clearly part of the question of dominance, we find it an adequate guide in an otherwise difficult area.

DPA is simple to administer, and can easily be used by any manager involved in innovation management. It provides a clear guide to convergence in a group (quantitative score), and provides us with a means to build synergistic groups (that is, to Mindmix) with a greater-than-average potential to find novel solutions.

Implications of the Brain Model for Managers

While the brain model gives an understanding of the physiological basis of cerebral differences, it is probably more important to concentrate on convergence and divergence. These are the thinking processes that are involved when you are working with people. At this practical end, for involvement with the innovative processes, a manager must:

- **Acknowledge everyone has a right brain,** including him- or herself. It may have been under-used, but it hasn't gone away. Some exercises in Part 2 may help you trigger this right brain into action. This is where the unusual, novel thoughts are hiding.

- **Recognise, respect and use divergent potential in others.** Much is talked in management about 'participation'. We're not sure what this means to you, but we do know people like to *be involved*, and are *more committed* to schemes or plans which they have had some involvement with in the development stage. And there's no easier way to involve people than ask for their ideas. Of course, for them this may mean overcoming years of ridicule and other depressors of divergence, but Chapters 3 and 4 should be useful here.

- **Accept odd ideas** – their novelty may just break through for you, and provide the innovative proposal you've been looking for. This is harder than it sounds, and requires you to keep an open mind. Idea-flows from divergent people are easily stopped, and self-control by the manager is imperative. The word 'No' is a major killer of ideas. Keep it under control. Chapters 3 and 4 discuss in detail some of the barriers to idea flow, and some of the behaviours required of managers who want to ensure idea flow.

- **Use the differing strengths of your people** – whether you use DPA or rely on your own knowledge of the strengths in a group, revealing these different strengths openly can create a synergy to make the group virtually one large super-brain. Chapter 4 discusses this aspect and should be of use to you.

- **Separate idea-evaluation from idea-generation** – clearly, and in time. Every attempt to evaluate closes down right-brain and divergent activity. When looking for ideas, don't evaluate. Leave evaluation until later. It's necessary, eventually, but not when ideas are young. Part 2 discusses this in more detail.

- **Be an objective evaluator, and let people know what has happened.** If your people helped by contributing ideas, they need to see what happened to their ideas. If you eliminate on subjective grounds, you'll have trouble feeding back. So make your criteria by which ideas are accepted or rejected as objective as possible, and make them visible enough to be an aid to communication. Chapters 4 and 8 will provide some clues here.

'Education is what survives when what has been learnt has been forgotten.'

B. F. Skinner

Test your divergent thinking with a crossword . . . and watch for the 'flash'.

ACROSS		DOWN	
1	A vegetable	1	A blow or hit
2	Female sheep	2	Judy's friend
3	Lays eggs	3	For making holes
4	Ocean	4	A party drink
5	For dropping			

1	2	3	4
2			
3			
4			
5			

In this chapter we have related convergent and divergent thinking to the now well-established notion of right-brain/left-brain dominance. We have also inferred that most of us, through the process of education, growing up, further education and work experience, develop thinking skills that are dominantly left-brain based. Our right brain, the source of

Here's an exercise about this book to stretch your own creativity. This book is about Mindmix, so we've subtitled each chapter as a M-I-X. For example, this one was 'Mental Inner Xcitement'.

You can no doubt do better. Try a few here:

M .... I .... X ....

M .... I .... X ....

M .... I .... X ....

much of our originality, is much neglected. Worse, those of us who *do* exercise some right-brain dominance tend not to be particularly sought after in normal places of work.

The implications for managers of this situation are clear: either remain left-brain dominant and stay idea-poor, or encourage more right-brain activity. We are not for a minute saying that, overall, right-brain activities should *replace* left brain, but if more divergent thinking is allowed into our work lives better ideas will certainly result. It's this growth of right-brain activity that is important. The outcome should be a much more productive, whole-brained manager and an idea-rich organisation.

Another view of individual differences of relevance to Mindmix:

Generating and accepting novelty necessarily imposes change. Managers, and others, respond to change in different ways.

Some react as **neophiliacs** – they seem to love change. As managers, they push for the adoption of new ideas. They act as agents for change. As group members, they eagerly grasp novelty, and enjoy divergence. Neophiliacs may not all be qualitative, right-brain, divergent thinkers. But if they're not, they certainly can be supportive of the efforts of divergent others.

Others react as **neophobiacs** – they seem to fear change. As managers, they are reluctant agents of change. They frequently reject new ideas on the basis of implementation difficulties. As group members, they do not participate well in 'wild' idea-generation. They prefer conservative answers.

A neophobiac managing a group of neophiliacs is seen as a conservative block. A neophiliac managing a group of neophobiacs may make group members particularly uncomfortable.

3

The Manager and Innovation

Managerial Innovative Xperiments

The Manager and Innovation

As a manager, you need do more than remain aware of the implications of convergent and divergent strengths. Such awareness by itself is not sufficient to move a park-bench tramp to a constructive and vocal pattern of behaviour, let alone move a group of them in that direction. And that is the situation for many managers.

Now . . . don't blame the tramps for their reticence; previous managers are responsible for a good deal of the tramp's behaviour. In other words, it's what managers **do** that directly affects innovative behaviour, not what they are aware of.

To produce innovative behaviour, the manager must deliberately manage the process of innovation. Certainly, this process is a recognisable entity (as mentioned in Chapter 2), with recognisable elements. These are more fully expanded in Part 2 but certainly the three major elements can be summarised as:

- **Generating ideas** . . . involving groups to provide new thoughts. Groups are simply more productive than any one individual member can be. (This is expanded in Chapter 7.)

- **Screening and evaluating ideas** ... again, involving groups, as the synergy available from different strengths (divergence *vs* convergence) simply means better decision-making. (This synergy concept is mentioned often. It's the basis of Mindmix. There's clarification in Chapter 8.)
- **Improving/protecting and planning the implementation of these ideas** ... again, involving groups, as both convergent and divergent contributions are required. (See Chapter 8.)

The common factor? *Groups.* And groups need effective structuring and leadership. The manager's key activities reduce to:

- Selecting people for team roles.
- Encouraging group synergy.
- Training ... both for knowledge (an overview perspective) and relevant skills.
- Communication and feedback procedures
- Overcoming the obstacles, some of which exist now and some of which will emerge as you get underway.

Selecting Team Members

How do you attract 'creative' people, and/or keep them once you've found them?

Creative people are supposedly attracted to creative environments. For a manager this means get your organisational innovative act together (see Chapter 4), and go out and beat your own drum. Tell people you have a creative environment. You'll also need to be able to detect the creative person. What and who is he or she? On page 46 is a list of what one major researcher has deduced about creative people. In the main, these are what we call *qualitative* things. The DPA (previously mentioned in Chapter 2), which distinguishes qualitative from quantitative preferences, can be useful here. It even detects, as a subpoint, a preference for being involved with new and different things (which the authors call a creative preference).

The fact is that everybody is creative, to some extent. They'll only show this in an environment where divergence is encouraged, where there's appropriate challenge and freedom, where their knowledge is relevant, and where they find opportunities in their job.

This last item of job opportunity is extremely important. Can you imagine a highly divergent individual in a job which demands convergence? Would you like your computer programmer to decide what information you need? Or would you like your weighbridge operator to decide on new ways to use the weighbridge? Probably not – but divergent people in such jobs would be frustrated, dissatisfied and generally cause you headaches.

The reverse is equally true; convergent people in jobs with divergent opportunity quite simply 'bomb out'. So, you've a marketing man who doesn't really come up with new programmes, who simply updates last year's programmes (who hasn't?)? Or a personnel manager who always advertises for new staff in the same newspaper, when what you really need is a greater range of applicants? The problems of lack of divergence are usually described as lack of imagination, and are around you everywhere each day.

The real question is 'horses for courses'. If you've jobs with qualitative opportunity, make sure you find people with qualitative potential. (You can measure this in both jobs and people.) If you don't, you have dissatisfied people. And asking a dissatisfied person for an idea on problem x will lead only to answers which address that person's primary problem . . . their job satisfaction. It's a sort of 'biased creativity'.

Keeping the right people in the right jobs is of itself a pathway to motivation. The research work with the DPA (see Further Reading if you're interested here) has been quite clear; productivity is increased where individuals fit the jobs they are in. And it's not such a big jump from convergence/divergence to quantitative/qualitative. One measure of productivity is surely

D. W. MacKinnon, *a researcher into creative talent, has described the creative person as:*

- Uninterested in small details.
- Concerned with the meanings and implications of data, rather than the facts for their own sake.
- Cognitively flexible.
- Verbally skilful.
- Open to his/her own feelings and emotions.
- Having a sensitive intellect/self-aware.
- Wide-ranging interests.
  (D. W. MacKinnon, 'The Nature & Nurture of Creative Talent', *American Psychologist*, Vol. XVII, No. 7, July 1960)

the flow and fluency of ideas, and the conversion rate of these to innovative and successful actions.

But the over-riding consideration with groups is (if you're after ideas, and it should be obvious that ideas are where innovation begins) to ensure you include some divergent minds in your groups or teams.

Encouraging Group Synergy

There are two types of groups of relevance in Mindmix and similar innovative activities; those which are essentially idea-generating groups, and those which are more total innovative groups.

'A camel is a racehorse designed by a committee', or so say the critics of groups as decision-makers. But groups do work; they have advantages in breadth of experience, varied knowledge, surfacing and confrontation of conflict and antagonism, and mutual support. In general, it has been shown that groups have an advantage where avoiding errors is of greater importance than speed. It has also been shown that most individuals increase their ability to make significant contributions in a group setting.

In idea-generating groups the need for divergent people and the need for right-brain accessing or tools for stimulating general divergence are obvious (and these tools are provided in Chapters 6 and 7). Such groups go under a variety of labels, such as productivity improvement teams, value analysis groups, creativity groups, idea groups, and so on. Popular in the recent past are groups under the heading quality circles, although such are not always exact copies of their Japanese parents.

> Good ideas don't just fade away. They're slaughtered by rampaging squads of carefully attired, analytical managers.

Within groups more deliberately designed for synergy – that is, to provide the Mindmix between divergent and convergent thinking – the need is for contributions from all types of thinkers. Such groups offer the potential for interdisciplinary effort. Providing that common visible processes are used, even a widely diverse group can be kept on a common track even when the group leader doesn't know where the track will lead.

Deliberately structured groups have an important role in the innovative process. But groups need leadership and the leader's role can be easily expanded to be the 'devil's advocate' for minority concepts, translating the layman's bright idea so that the scientist can see it really does answer his problem, or stopping the convergent thinkers from killing an intuitive idea

> 'The problem is to find a form of association that will defend and protect with the whole common force the person and good of each associate, and in which each, while uniting himself with all, may still obey himself alone and remain as free as before'.
>
> Rousseau, *The Social Contract*

too early which as voiced doesn't have a leg to stand on (but might grow some, given time), etc. Groups not only have a role, but must be managed and used purposefully to achieve success-ful innovative outcomes. Obviously, it's the responsibility of an innovative manager to create this synergy with his or her and other groups.

The 'how to do it' is scattered throughout this book. It's the basic Mindmix message. The core of the answer for the indi-vidual manager is:

- Identify the divergent/convergent skills and abilities within team members.
- Establish the legitimacy of divergent thinking in the group.
- Introduce team members to the idea of differing strengths: 'Jack's our quantitative resource. Mary's our qualitative resource. She can give us some way-out ideas. But that's okay . . . Jack will question them.'
- Use the idea-generating tools. (You'll be exposed to plenty of these in Chapters 6 and 7.)
- Communicate openly about successes and failures, provid-ing the reasons/rationale for each.

Training Group Members

If we acknowledge that the organisation is a triangular hier-archy, it's not too difficult to see that the bottom of the triangle is (superficially) the best place to generate ideas. There are probably more divergent heads there. There are certainly usually more heads there. So, generating ideas at the bottom can mean an increased flow of ideas upwards – if you capitalise on this resource.

How? Train them to use the idea-generating tools. The intent is not to increase individual creativity (that's a doubtful con-cept), but rather to provide comfort with processes. This comfort is necessary; people asked to play with tools to which they are unaccustomed don't maximise the output from their use.

And maximising the output is what you're after. In idea generation, quantity precedes quality as an intent. Repeatedly we talk about **delaying evaluation** or suspending judgment. Evaluation and judgment are where quality counts. At the generation end, it's quantity of ideas you want . . . so train your people to become accustomed to the tools.

Train them also in how to work together. This is easier than it sounds. It was referred to in the previous section (as synergy). Make people aware of the different strengths and the mutual advantage available from acknowledging these strengths. They'll respond. We've seen it too many times to doubt it. 'Gee, I didn't know Jack was like that' and similar comments are normal.

Educate your people to see that the pursuit of a 'better' solution might require a very novel answer, but that this novelty is legitimate. 'It's okay around here to throw up your oddest thought!'

And one last thought on training: train yourself! You've really started this process or you wouldn't be reading about Mindmix.

Communications and Feedback

This is more fully covered in the next chapter, as it's really an organisational phenomenon. But it's also the individual manager's responsibility. It simply means:

- Talk to your people about innovation, about novelty, about the respectability of the very unusual. Refer to breakthroughs and examples of obvious divergence from other industries – stories such as: cardiologist Garrett Lee got the idea for a revolutionary new technique to use laser beams to melt fatty deposits that clog arteries from a movie. He saw Obi-Wan Kenobi using a laser sword in *Star Wars*.

- Explain criteria you're using to assess/evaluate ideas, especially when you're feeding back about acceptance or rejection. (And remember, this is some time *after* idea generation.) In other words, explain the rationale of rejection . . . not just a 'No'.

Obstacles to Innovation

'There are no barriers to creativity – only obstacles to surmount.'

If you were asked what you would need to have happen at work so that you could become truly innovative, what would you say? Probably something like:

'Give me a *real* opportunity –'

'Listen to my ideas.'

'Give me a chance to develop my ideas. Support me!'

'Take a punt on my hunch.'

'Don't try to make me fit the mould. Give me some room to move.'

'Look beyond the immediate disruption my efforts may cause, and the risk, and consider longer-term benefits.'

'Indulge me in my fantasies – at least some of the time.'

'Let me try it, even if I fail.'

'Provide a fair reward for success.'

'Allow me my idiosyncracies, my peculiarities.'

'Don't put my ideas down too quickly . . . give yourself time to get used to them.'

'Don't judge my ideas by my position; I may be junior, but I've got a brain.'

'Don't laugh at my ideas.'

Responses like these illustrate the obstacles that get in the way of creativity at work. The obstacles affect us as individuals. They close down our right-brain wanderings. They affect total organisations – no one is prepared to 'lead with their chin'; it's too dangerous or it's not expected. Conservatism of this rigid kind is common throughout our society, influencing each of us to some degree.

MANAGERS AND FAILURES

In a recent survey by the US Institute of Public Administration of innovative failure (new ideas not reaching the marketplace) it was found that management ineptitude accounted for almost 25 per cent of such failures; it was only marginally less important as a 'failure factor' than market rejection. In terms of less publicised 'ideas', those either pre-product or related to the human or financial resources of organisations, it is likely this figure is even higher. But even as it is, the consequences of one in four good but novel ideas being either rejected or insufficiently supported are easy to visualise in today's setting, and they may be even more competitively disastrous in the near future.

Ideas are born inside the heads of individuals. Ideas are very fragile at birth and easily destroyed. They are like seeds of a plant; full of potential to grow if given the right setting, the right nourishment, and the right climate. But they're easily killed off, just the same. A young idea needs to be given enough early support to avoid the dangers of the organisational environment, to get its head out above ground. Without this early support no one has much of a chance to see what it really looks like.

With a little time, the idea will strengthen, if it's healthy. It can then offer its organisational owners a better view of its potential profitability or other benefits, and better stand the scrutiny of the managers and committees who might have a stake in it. New ideas have to survive in the face of a host of other organisational activities and priorities. Many managers and bosses are good at saying 'No', and many a divergent thinker comes to the conclusion that discretion may be the better part of innovation! So it's not easy. But identifying the obstacles offers a chance of overcoming them, and building stronger divergent skills in the organisation.

A number of things hold us back as individuals. Here are some major ones.

FEAR

Fear acts as a major suppressant of novel ideas. As individuals we fear ridicule, we fear being rejected, we fear losing prestige or being branded as 'odd'. These are all very real. In our management development activities we often ask groups to list the factors that cause them to hold back from offering their views in meetings and similar work situations. Each person usually offers several reasons, but almost two thirds of all reasons offered are directly associated with this single barrier – fear of ridicule, fear of being put down, fear of being seen as inadequate. Obviously, this fear is likely to limit the flow of new, original or unconventional ideas; it will *certainly* reduce the number offered publicly in either group or one-to-one settings.

Each of us knows we're capable of some particularly peculiar thoughts. We've all had what at first seemed like brilliant ideas.

A WHOLE-BRAIN APPROACH

A couple of suggestions from a study of how managers think: managers should

'. . . offset tendencies to be rational by stressing the importance of values and preferences, of using imagination, and of acting with an incomplete picture of the situation.'

'. . . bolster intuition with rational thinking. Recognise that good intuition requires hard work, study, periods of concentrated thought, and rehearsal.'

Daniel Isenberg, Assistant Professor, Harvard Graduate School of Business, in 'How Managers Think', *Harvard Business Review*, Nov.–Dec. 1984.

But most of us have forgotten more of them than we can count. Why? Because we never actually put them into words to share with others. We self-censored. We dropped them without having to run the risk of ridicule.

A QUICK TEST OF THE POWER OF RIDICULE

When you are next chairing a meeting, speaking to a group, or talking at a conference, ask the people there to consider what things most hold them back from voicing their thoughts or offering their comments and ideas in group situations or meetings.

Give them some slips on which to write their responses, anonymously (one response per slip), and ask them to complete the task in 3 minutes. Then gather up the slips, and while you're getting on with the major purpose of the meeting/seminar/conference, have someone sort the slips into categories.

Over half the responses will be things like 'I might be laughed at/put down/thought silly/made to feel embarrassed.'

Ridicule, real or imagined, is the enemy of creative ideas. And fear of ridicule is very widespread.

BREAKING THROUGH THE FEAR OF RIDICULE

Create a climate where the value of the 'odd' divergent idea is appreciated – then others won't laugh, they'll enquire instead. This requires education of your groups so that everyone sees the pursuit of a 'better' solution – and the novelty which that might imply – as legitimate. It also requires that all who are involved understand the innovative intent, and the philosophy behind it. Again, 'education' is the key to establishing this innovative mind set.

Educate your people about left brain-right brain differences and convergent-divergent processes. Let them see that everybody else has the same hang-ups . . . but we can beat it.

What else can you do?

● Eliminate opportunities for ridicule. Use non-verbal techniques until a group is used to offering the unusual. In

Chapter 6 a slip-writing technique is described. This technique makes an individual's contribution anonymous. No one can laugh at *me* for my 'funny' but clever idea, because the origin is unknown.

● Encourage unusual ideas by offering them. If you can overcome the fear of ridicule in yourself, you'll present an example to those you work with.

HABIT

Our daily routines constrain us. We look at familiar products, familiar people with familiar eyes. We hear with familiar ears. 'He or she has never had any decent ideas before. Why should I listen especially hard to this one?' We think only of the short term, of today's business, when we often need to think more about tomorrow's opportunities. It adds up to us not looking for innovation unless we have to. Change disrupts, and that is usually uncomfortable.

Not all habits are bad, but unthinking habitual behaviour is ingenuity's worst enemy. We all get into ruts without realising it. We tend to do the same thing in the same way at the same time each day. Our approaches to people, problems and opportunities become predictable. The mystery and challenge a person had when the job was new give way to secure routines.

The power of habit in our thinking is revealed by the following exercise. Read it, and count the times the letter 'f' appears. Then ask friends or family to do the same. Then consider why the answers differ (they usually do). It's 'habit' again.

FINISHED FEATURES ARE THE RESULT OF YEARS OF FILM-MAKERS FORAGING, COMBINED WITH THE EXPERIENCE OF MANY WRITERS, PRODUCERS AND FINANCIAL EXPERTS.

The power of habit is exemplified in this example. We were recently working with a group looking for a novel packaging/

presentation for a new product. A small subgroup was asked to sort approximately three hundred ideas that had been generated. They went away, and returned from this task with only about 80 ideas, neatly sorted into categories. When asked where the remaining 220 ideas were, they described them as 'rejects'. The subsequent discussion revealed that all the completely odd, and therefore the potentially novel, ideas had been included with the rejects because 'we just don't do it that way here'. Fortunately, we were able to recover the 220 ideas (literally, from the dustbin). And yes, one of these ideas was later developed into a viable option. So even in this instance, where a deliberately creative exercise was under way, habit took over, not consciously, not deliberately, but just as effectively.

OVERCOMING HABIT

As with fear, education and understanding of the process of innovation is the first step. Personal resolution is another ('I *will* develop a different view of this'), aided by some objective setting to strengthen the resolution ('I'll develop *two* different views by Friday next week'). Consciously breaking your routines can help. Decide to drive to work a different way and *do it*. Choose a new, unknown restaurant for your next meal out and *go there*. Invite new people from another relevant department to your next meeting, and *involve them*. Identify your least important meeting and *don't go*. Buy a tie of a colour you've never worn!

What else can you do?

- Accept your own divergent thoughts as normal, and realise that habits, while comfortable (you don't have to think much when behaviour is habitual) are not going to assist divergent thinking. Break a few habits! And show others that you have done so.
- Borrow a point of view from far away. Approaching situations from a different point of view can help. For example, ask how an ancient Egyptian or Greek (or any

contemporary culture with which you're familiar) might view the problem.

- Borrow a point of view from close at hand. Using someone else's point of view can sometimes jolt you out of a rut. Perhaps a co-worker, or someone in your family. Imagine what it's like to wake up in the morning for that person. What are the impressions, what responses to things in the room, reactions to morning routines? What lies ahead for the day? What objectives or events will bring joy? What will bring upset? Seeing with a child's eyes is particularly challenging, but it often brings startling new perceptions.

- Confront the difficult. We're warned a lot about stress. But stress can be creative. Taking a problem which has been simmering on the back-burner for months, or has been hiding in the 'too-hard' file, and calling for an open confrontation can bring fresh perspectives to all involved.

- Practise spontaneity. Many people lack a healthy sense of 'letting-the-hair-down-in-public'. Developed nations have few customs which enforce spontaneity, so each person must develop his or her own forms. Start by talking to people in lifts.

- Try new hobbies, different recreational activities, simple rearrangements of furniture, different routes to the office, lunches with different people. Variety spurs novelty and ingenuity. Even taking time to play challenging games, solve intriguing puzzles or read science fiction can alert the mind to new possibilities. Exercise can clear mental cobwebs.

The human brain has an incredible capacity for rejecting new information.

My brain is guilty of this –
☐ rarely   ☐ sometimes   ☐ often   ☐ too often

(Tick one)

PREJUDICE

Sometimes we automatically reject ideas against which we have an emotional bias. At other times, we don't consider some alternatives because a favourite method, material or person is involved in one of the alternatives so that is the one which we quickly see as 'good' or 'worthwhile'.

Both these forms of prejudice cause us to judge ideas prematurely. A new idea is like a plant which needs time to grow, and premature judgment is like trampling on the plant as soon as the first green shoot shows against the soil. At this stage the plant, like the new idea, is defenceless. The idea has not yet had the chance, or the time, to be improved and reach a stage where it can sensibly be examined more critically.

Premature judgment, often seen by workmates as the instinctive knockback or the knee-jerk reaction, is the death of divergent thinking. If people see their ideas are just not being

seriously considered, then they have no strong reason to keep making suggestions. Psychologically, they just go and sit on a park bench. They swallow their resentment, reduce their commitment, and join the ranks of the thousands of other apathetic employees who have been similarly treated. The only difference between this group of people and the thousands of others is that these are *your* people, driven away by *your* tendency to make premature judgments or snap decisions. Innovation cannot flourish in such a climate.

Premature judgment can be less than deliberate. It's as if we, as managers, had a language set that separates us from all others. For example, have you heard a van driver say 'It's not in the budget!' Probably not. But you've heard managers' knee-jerk responses given to unusual thoughts. There are a few of them on page 59. Of course, they stop the flow of ideas from our people . . . usually with a thump!

PREMATURE JUDGMENT

At a recent creative decision-making seminar held for a client with transportation of food and beverage domestic delivery interests, a group member offered an idea about improving the delivery vans. 'That would cost too much,' said someone, dropping a common killer phrase on the embryonic idea. And this 'murderer' then tried to move on quickly to some other concept. Fortunately, a strong personality in the group was able to intervene. 'Hang on,' said he, 'let's hear more about the idea.'

It turned out that the idea was for a simple but distinctive facelift for the vans, at a cost that would probably be very modest. What eventually happened is not important here, but it illustrates our eternal readiness to jump too early on others' ideas.

If you don't believe it, watch for how frequently it happens at the next meeting you attend! And then act to give innovation a chance by asking the originator of the idea to tell the group more about it.

It might just be the beginning of something creative and worthwhile.

OVERCOMING PREJUDICE

What can you do to overcome prejudice? Follow one of the basic rules for encouraging divergent thinking: *suspend* judgment. It's ideas first, lots of them, even the wild ones. Evalu-

---

IDEA KILLERS
Don't be ridiculous!
It costs too much!
That's outside our area!
We don't have the time!
It's not *our* problem!
Let's get back to reality!
You're ahead of your time!
It's not in the budget!
Has someone else tried it?
It's too hard to sell!
Let's form a committee!
That will make other things out-of-date!
You can't teach an old dog new tricks!
Let's shelve it for the time being!
That needs more market research!
It's a good idea in principle, but . . .
We've tried it before!
It can't be done!
It's too big a change!
We're too small!
Are you serious?
I've never done it before!
Why change it . . . it's working!
We're not ready for that!
Everyone will laugh at us!
We did all right without it!
It won't work here!
Management wouldn't go for it!
Customers wouldn't go for it!
The union wouldn't go for it!
London won't like it!

Add some more:

_____

_____

_____

_____

_____

_____

ation comes later. This takes practice, but it's possible. In idea groups, make it possible for the group to control premature judgment. Make it acceptable for members to point out when ideas are reacted to prematurely (and almost always negatively). Say: 'Hold it, Jack — you're judging. That comes later.' Some brainstorming groups even give members red cards, or flags, to hold up silently when they hear judgmental comments.

Early judgment often comes from those who are the company 'knockers', although 'knockers' have no monopoly on such behaviour. If possible, leave them out of your ideas sessions. They have a valuable part to play later, when the evaluation stage has begun, because of their ability to see flaws. So involve them, but at this later stage when their type of contribution is appropriate — not in the early days when ideas are too easily killed.

Drop 'Idea Killers' from your vocabulary . . . or at least control your use of them. Learn to delay: it's critical.

SOCIALISATION

The processes of growing up and of education all strongly reinforce our left-brain, rational processes. Comment has already been made on this in Chapter 2 and is supported by statements such as follows from an eminent educationalist: 'we still do a brutal job of squelching such [questioning] tendencies. We have perfected many devices of ridicule and evasion for putting the curious child in his place.'[1] Experiments in some schools support the force of this statement.

At one East Coast American school, children were allowed to spend half their time in art classes and the other half doing conventional subjects. Result? Their performance in maths and science and many other subjects increased. Work in other schools in other countries confirms this. The extra effort and time put into developing right-brain skills helps build left-brain competence also. One outcome is a more 'whole-brained' person.

Too few efforts have been expended in this direction. To

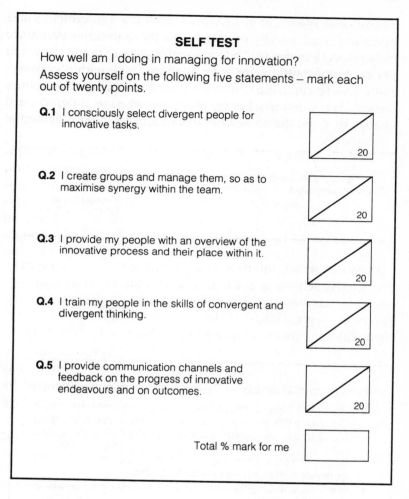

SELF TEST

How well am I doing in managing for innovation?

Assess yourself on the following five statements – mark each out of twenty points.

Q.1 I consciously select divergent people for innovative tasks.

20

Q.2 I create groups and manage them, so as to maximise synergy within the team.

20

Q.3 I provide my people with an overview of the innovative process and their place within it.

20

Q.4 I train my people in the skills of convergent and divergent thinking.

20

Q.5 I provide communication channels and feedback on the progress of innovative endeavours and on outcomes.

20

Total % mark for me

quote Gardener C. Quarton: 'some techniques for modifying behaviour are relatively reversible (drugs, prosthesis), others are in some sense irreversible (destructive brain operations, college education).[2] Quarton's grouping of 'destructive brain operations' and 'college education' is probably not accidental, particularly with respect to the divergent skills associated with creative thinking. Let's review just a little research: the US educational system at high school level is often criticised as being less academically oriented than those in other Western cultures, yet a measure of educational objectives found only 1.7 per cent of the total were to be at all involved with divergent skills. This research is a bit dated – it took place in the 'swinging sixties'. We wonder whether there has been any significant change through the somewhat less radical 1970s and 1980s?

'Help people develop their full potential. Catch them doing something right.'

Blanchard, K., and Johnson, S., *The One-Minute Manager*;
Fontana/Collins, 1983.

Pressures which interfere with the creative process are not restricted to schooling and education. Social pressures at home and in the community also push us towards conformity. Some parents go to great lengths to instil conventional behaviour into their children, 'for the child's good', or because it's 'good man-

---

Even the best ideas can be 'held down' by convergent forces:

- Chester F. Carlson proved his invention of Xerography on 22 October 1938. He had even refined it to an automatic copier by 1940. But Xerography was not presented to the public until 22 October 1948 by the Halrid Company (later to become Xerox Corporation). Chester Carlson could not generate earlier interest in his 'wild' idea.
- The first 'traffic lights' were installed outside the Houses of Parliament, Westminster, in 1868. There was a fatal accident. No one was interested for many years ('too dangerous'). The next reported use of signals was in Cleveland in 1914, only four years short of a half-century later.
- King Camp Gillette invented the modern disposable shaving blade in 1895. It took until 1903 to get any into the market place. The idea was widely blocked . . . no one could make steel thin enough, flat enough, sharp enough, hard enough, cheap enough. At least, not until they asked 'how'.

ners', or for a host of other apparently sensible reasons. The result, nevertheless, is that the child so treated learns to avoid right-brain thoughts because they bring him or her no praise, no recognition, no sense of well-being. Those nice feelings come only when conventional left-brain behaviour is volunteered. Some researchers suggest that these social and family pressures result in most of our children having had most of the creativity 'educated out of them' by the time they are 8 or 9 years old.

OVERCOMING ADVERSE EFFECTS OF SOCIALISATION

What can the individual manager do? Well, for a start it's probably not possible to reverse 20 or 30 years of socialisation. But you can make percentage gains. Here are a few ideas:

- Try to reverse the emphasis on convergent skills.
  How?
  – Become an example to your people. Model the divergent skills that are appropriate. Communicate the successes.
  – Encourage divergent thinking. Make interactive 'idea' sessions part of the normal working day. Schedule the first one now.
  – Accept the 'odd' ideas from your people. Show that judgment *can* be suspended by witholding your own.
- Create an environment where divergent thinking is made respectable. Not just condoned. Not just encouraged. It has to be made legitimate!
  How?
  – Accept differences, especially differences of approach, and different ideas and possible answers. Be an example again. Visibly recognise effort, even when solutions are not forthcoming or ideas are not necessarily 'winners'. Divergent thinking is no guarantee of success – but it usefully changes the odds in your favour. And don't punish failure. Seeking novel solutions is not risk free. Punish failure, and most people stop trying.
- Build awareness in your group of left brain-right brain differences, and convergent-divergent processes. Make

divergent ways of thinking visible, understood, and seen as respectable.

How?

– Begin an 'ideas' session with an explanation. Add credibility by finding examples of successful or constructive divergent thinking in your company's or department's recent history. Or start by having members of your team read this book. Perhaps use slip-writing, a simple technique described in Chapter 7, to gather ideas from your people on how better to use the Mindmix approach.

– DPA technology, mentioned in Chapter 2, also offers a way to make public different approaches to problem solving and decision making within a group. The very fact that the differences *are* public aids both understanding and acceptance of them.

- Train your team to use Mindmix methods, and build skills in divergent thinking. Help them meld both convergent and divergent skills into a whole-brained approach to managing their opportunities.

How?

– First, keep reading this book. Then follow the activities suggested by identifying, with your team, an open-ended problem which is important, and which needs a solution. Don't start by choosing the toughest problem on your list; remember one of your objectives is to build team confidence in divergent skills. But don't go for a trivial issue, either. Then use some of the methods in Chapter 7 to open up right-brain processes. Chapter 9 offers a detailed approach to this whole question of making it happen.

- You will soon reach a situation where ideas are flowing. Some will be better than others. You will accept some, and back them, but reject others. What's important here is to provide feed-back to the group about why some ideas have been accepted, and others not. It's especially important with a rejected idea that people *know* why it was not accepted.

THE CALF PATH

One day, through the primeval wood,
A calf walked home, as good calves
    should;
But made a trail all bent askew,
A crooked trail as all calves do.
Since then two hundred years have
    fled,
And, I infer, the calf is dead.
But still he left behind his trail,
And thereby hangs my moral tale.

The trail was taken up next day
By a lone dog that passed that way;
And then a wise bell-wether sheep
Pursued the trail o'er vale and steep,
And drew the flock behind him too,
As good bell-wethers always do.

And from that day o'er hill and glade,
Through those old woods a path was
    made;
And many men wound in and out,
And dodged and turned and bent
    about
And uttered words of righteous wrath
Because 'twas such a crooked path.
But still they followed – do not laugh –
The first migrations of that calf,
And through this winding wood-way
    stalked,
Because he wobbled when he
    walked.

This forest path became a lane,
That bent and turned and turned
    again,
This crooked lane became a road,
Where many a poor horse with his
    load
Toiled on beneath the burning sun,
And travelled some three miles in one,
And thus a century and a half
They trod the footsteps of that calf.

The years passed on in swiftness
    fleet,
The road became a village street;
And this before men were aware,

A city's crowded thoroughfare,
And soon the central street was
    this
Of a renowned metropolis;
And men two centuries and a half
Trod in the footsteps of that calf.

Each day a hundred thousand
    rout,
Followed this zig-zag calf about;
And o'er crooked journey went
The traffic of a continent.

A hundred thousand men were led
By one calf near three centuries
    dead,
They followed still his crooked
    way,
And lost one hundred years a day;
For thus such reverence is lent
To well-established precedent.

A moral lesson this might teach,
Were I ordained and called to
    preach;
For men are prone to go it blind
Along the calf-paths of the mind,
And work away from sun to sun,
To do what other men have done.

They follow in the beaten track,
And out and in, and forth and
    back,
And still their devious course
    pursue,
To keep the path that others do,
They keep the path a sacred
    groove,
Along which all their lives they
    move.

And how the wise old wood-gods
    laugh,
Who saw the first primeval calf;
Ah! many things this tale might
    teach
But I am not ordained to preach.

Sam Walker Foss, 1895

How do you do this?
— By telling your people your reasons for acceptance or rejection. The simplest and most convincing way to do this is to make public within the team the decision *criteria* you use. Better still, develop the criteria jointly with team members so that they are shared and understood from the outset. However you do it, communicating your reasons is vital. People will accept that their ideas were not 'winners' if they can understand where they fell short. This is where the criteria are so valuable (and there's more on this in Chapter 8). It's only when the 'Thanks Jill, but we're not going ahead with that one' comes with *no* reasoned explanation that Jill starts to wonder whether it's all worthwhile. If you provide reasons, and if they are fair ones, most people will accept a decision without losing too much enthusiasm.

4

The Organisation and Innovation

Managing Innovative Xcitement

The Organisation and Innovation

How do organisations become innovative? What's the impact of innovative processes, such as Mindmix, on the normal smooth-running of your organisation? How do you safely and easily intrude Mindmix, whole or part, into your already busy schedule?

Almost every organisation with which we've worked has made claims about innovative intents. 'Of course we're into innovation; that's the name of the game.' But frequently their actions don't hold up even to superficial scrutiny. Many of the obstacles to innovation described earlier are alive and well and living in the would-be innovative organisation.

A commitment to innovation implies much more than merely wanting to innovate. It imposes responsibilities on management and the organisation which should not be seen as additive, but are the full measure of so-called 'management responsibilities'. An innovative intent is clearly the starting point (as shown on the schematic on page 69) but is clearly not sufficient for innovation to occur.

Creativity in organisations is sometimes manifested accidentally and sometimes deliberately. An example of the former is
the machine operator who makes an unrecorded modification,
which he found to work rather than made work, to his machine
and achieves some particular result (increased output, easier
operation). An example of the latter is the R & D scientist who
discovers a new technology in response to demand, or the
designer who invents a new product to use this technology. But
whether accidental or deliberate, both are innovations. As we
said earlier (Chapter 1) innovation in the broadest sense
includes the idea of invention and discovery, but goes beyond
it. It is anything that provides unique solutions to problems,
opportunities or challenges – whether large or small.

The internal innovative capability of an organisation is a
resource. It cannot be measured as accurately as the size of the
labour force, or the capacity of a plant, or the amount of capital
assets. But all forms of resource are measured in approxi-
mation; capital assets as a 'book value' are usually quite
different from what might actually be realised in a reinvest-
ment situation; labour force size does not really tell much as to
the quality of that labour force.

But despite difficulties of measurement, this innovative
resource exists. If one takes the viewpoint that the future is the
primary concern of a manager, then it might be argued that in
terms of resource management a manager's primary responsibility concerns the effective use of the innovative potential
available to him.

Steering a steady course through the storms of business based
on successful patterns of the past is naturally a sound approach
for top management. But also having the ability to respond to
severe squalls and calms, and being able to capitalise on the
opportunities presented by very favourable winds, is a real
need. There are several things a manager can do to manage the
internal innovative resource to satisfy this need. Many of these
were discussed in Chapter 3. They revolve around three key
variables: the individual, the organisation itself, and the processes employed within the organisation. Some of the indi-

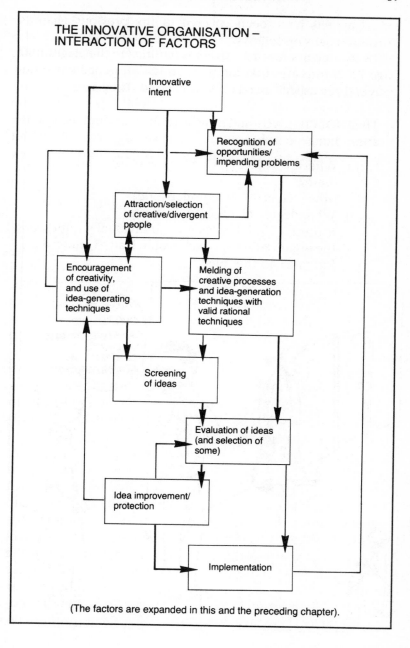

THE INNOVATIVE ORGANISATION –
INTERACTION OF FACTORS

Innovative
intent

Recognition of
opportunities/
impending problems

Attraction/selection
of creative/divergent
people

Encouragement
of creativity,
and use of
idea-generating
techniques

Melding of
creative processes
and idea-generation
techniques with
valid rational
techniques

Screening
of ideas

Evaluation of ideas
(and selection of
some)

Idea improvement/
protection

Implementation

(The factors are expanded in this and the preceding chapter).

vidual aspects have been covered in the previous chapter. Further expansion follows.

The framework for this chapter is outlined in the diagram on page 71. It indicates that for an organisation to become innovative, three aspects need to be addressed. They are:

1. The **INDIVIDUAL** – and how he or she fits with the organisation. In particular,

   (a) What level of ROLE CLARITY as to innovative input is there?
       How well is this role understood?
   (b) What degree of VALUES fit exists?
       Is there a clash between the individual's values, and the organisation's, which would lead to reduced performance in the role?

MANAGEMENT'S ROLE

RECOGNISE

INDIVIDUAL

Convergent and divergent talent and use where possible in groups to

Attract creative people
Person/job mix: 'horses for courses'
Identify/motivate/encourage the divergent thinker

Encourage 'whole brain' recognition/activities

VIEW THE

ORGANISATION

Dynamically to

Develop a conducive culture
Minimise unnecessary bureaucracy

Encourage synergistic (Mindmix) groups

COMMUNICATE, IMPLANT AND MAKE VISIBLE THE

NECESSARY PROCESSES

based on knowledge and skills to

MIX

for synergy

(right brain)

Accessing processes for stimulating, generating intuition and novelty

(left brain)

Use rational processes to evaluate, choose, plan

Then, FEEDBACK!

(c) What are the individual's PREFERENCES for various job activities, and what are the activities required by the job?
How well do personal preferences and job requirements fit?
Poor fit, where the job requires people to carry out tasks they don't like, leads to poor performance levels in that job.

(d) What REWARD system exists, to link the person's endeavours to the organisation's goals?

All of the above provide a link between the organisation and each individual in it.

2. The **ORGANISATION** – in particular, what resources does it provide? These resources fall into several categories:

(e) The PHYSICAL environment, especially the tools or technical aids or technology necessary for effective performance.

(f) The GROUP environment, especially with regard to compatibility, complementary skills, and potential for synergy.

(g) The ORGANISATIONAL environment – in particular its *structure*, and how that structure supports an innovative intent, and the *culture* that is created.

3. The **PROCESSES** associated with building innovative responses and reinforcing them.
What processes are understood/used/reinforced?

This chapter now explores each of these in turn.

1. The Individual

(a) ORGANISATIONAL ROLE AND ROLE CLARITY
What does 'Part of your job is to be creative – be innovative' really mean?

If you *do* have that interesting idea, what do you do about it? Do you create a report, talk to your boss, file it, take it to the committee, or set about making it work yourself? If you don't know – if your role is unclear – it's unlikely that you'll be effective.

And how much time is available for the thinking necessary for real innovation? We all know the

> **THINK**

sign on the office wall. How does a boss react when he or she passes an open office door and sees someone gazing at the ceiling? Boss stops, looks and says ... what? It might be 'Thinking again, eh? Good! You've had some useful ideas this year.' Or it might be, in many organisations, something less flattering, said with or without a smile.

The point is, role clarity is more than just *your* understanding of your role – it's a mutual understanding that's required between you, your manager, and other involved colleagues. And if time for thinking is not part of that role expectation, innovative behaviour will be hard to find.

Further, do those same role expectations allow innovative thoughts to be expressed? Remember that 'innovative' often equals strange, bizarre, odd, or apparently foolish. If this acceptance of the 'strange' is not part of your role, and part of others, then 'put-down', knee-jerk reactions from others follow the voicing of the idea ... and that's often the end of it. Back you go to your own particular park-bench!

Role clarity needs to be openly acknowledged as a prerequisite. Be careful not to confuse 'precisely defined tasks' with 'role clarity'. Detailed definition of what is to be done is **NOT** the need. That would be counterproductive, because it would constrain people.

The need is for clear understanding that innovative activity is actively sought – and that sometimes this will lead to less-than-conventional behaviour and output. But that is just what

innovation is about! It's about being different, at least some of
the time.

Acceptable role clarity exists when this is understood,
accepted and constructively built upon. The 'Killer Phrases'
listed in Chapter 3 are clear indications of innovative roles
simply not being understood.

(b) VALUES – INDIVIDUAL AND ORGANISATIONAL

Values are a fundamental sense of what is 'right' and what is
'wrong'. People clearly hold to particular values – they have a
'value system'. It commonly contains these deeply held beliefs
about morality, democracy, religion, ecology, etc. Organisations also have value systems: they believe certain things are
right ('We make explosives for industry') while other things are
wrong ('We do not make ammunition for the military'). The
values stance here might be: mining is right, war is wrong.
Where individuals in that company share these values, then
there is no values-conflict; 'values' do not get in the way of
individual performance. Where the values are not shared,
where an individual may be opposed to mining, perhaps in
certain areas of the country, then clearly that individual would
be uncomfortable, and likely to perform at less than peak levels.
Such individuals would normally not seek employment with
that company, so you may say 'Where's the problem?' The
problem often arises when organisations change their strategic
direction or change course; or if you like, shift their values
position.

(c) PREFERENCES – INDIVIDUAL 'LIKES' AND JOB
DEMANDS

The wrong person in the right job (or however you like to
express it) presents an obstacle. If a position has a divergent
potential but it's filled by a convergent individual, then you've
a problem.

Jobs can be measured to determine the extent to which they
demand quantitative or qualitative cerebral preferences. This
measure has been demonstrated by the work of Drs Kable and

Hicks and the DPA concepts referred to earlier in Chapter 2. Their research shows clearly that the closer an individual's cerebral preference profile is to the quantitative/qualitative split of the job, the more likely it will be that the person will be satisfied in the job.

People who are in inappropriate jobs for their preference profiles manifest the symptoms of job dissatisfaction. They complain. They absent themselves. They fight against the 'injustices' (at least, those which affect them). And they expend their efforts and energy on trying to make the job fit their preference profile. Such people's creative potential is lost to the organisation as a whole. It's being used either to 'beat the system' or to redesign the system for their own comfort.

Job satisfaction is not a sufficient condition for idea contribution. But a certain, minimum level is a necessary condition. There's no point in asking an unhappy group to give you new product ideas; they're still thinking up ideas to damage you (the system). But a group with a relatively good fit with their job (that is, the right horses for the right courses) may just be able to give you what you want. Manage the 'fit' if you want people to really contribute.

(d) REWARDS

Motivation, and the rewards people seek, are complex questions. There are probably thousands of motives or things which 'switch people on'. Many researchers feel that at least three motives affect most if not all people at work. These are power, affiliation and achievement. People who have a high power motive require rewards which satisfy this need – they like to prevail over others and get reward from being in charge. People who have a high affiliation motive like to be with others, and are rewarded from just such opportunities. People who have a high achievement motive like to see a job completed, to see results . . . and thus like to get feedback of attainment, as this is in itself rewarding.

These motives clearly affect behaviour – in fact, behaviour is possibly the only real clue to motivation. For example, someone who tells you they want to be the world champion tennis player but does nothing towards this supposed goal is clearly not motivated (at least, not to becoming the world champion; he or she is clearly motivated to talk with you, which suggests affiliation rather than achievement). And this behaviour, and the rewards associated with it, places three obstacles to creativity in organisations.

The first problem to overcome relates to the appropriateness of rewards. If an offered reward (e.g. an incentive) is inappropriate to my dominant motive, or I can't see or haven't learnt an association which makes it relevant, then it doesn't affect my behaviour. I don't consciously strive to convert the potential reward (incentive) into an actual reward. There's not much use offering me money for ideas if what I really want is to be seen as important (that is, power-motivated). Of course, I may have learnt 'money is power'. Some idea-generation programmes are based on incentives and do exactly this. They assume everybody is attracted by the same potential reward. And, what may be even worse, some idea-generation programmes offer no visible reward at all!

The second problem relates to group behaviour. Groups are vital to idea-generation activities (Chapter 7 will expand this).

'DON'T FORGET WHO'S IN CHARGE HERE!'

'Nobody's going to pull the wool over *my* eyes with talk of these crazy ideas.' Managers who think and feel like this have stopped listening. And if they've been not listening consistently for a year, then their people have stopped offering novelty in their ideas. They will have gone back to offering what they know is acceptable (but unexciting), because they've become tired of being put down just so their boss can feel that he or she is 'really in charge here'. Overt concern for status kills innovation. If a manager can't handle the thought of having his or her apparent status and 'authority' challenged by competent, creative group members, then any innovation responsibilities should be handed over to someone who has less trouble in putting personal needs aside while they listen to their people.

But groups which are controlled only casually provide a rewarding experience only for people with a high affiliation motive. Achievement-motivated participants may well feel it's a waste of time. Groups which are heavily structured tend to provide opportunities for status reinforcement, which is rewarding to the power-motivated individuals. Good group leadership skills become important, and the lack of these skills creates an obstacle.

The third problem is that going to work is for many the dullest part of their life. Work is simply not that exciting. Even where the 'right horse is on the right course', contribution is limited if rewards appropriate to motives are not offered. For too many people work structures:

- Ignore the affiliative motive; opportunities for friendly discussion are few.
- Are typically contrary to the achievement motive; challenges are too small, and no one tells the individual how well (towards a goal) he or she has done.
- Are antagonistic to the power motive; very few have the luxury of being made to feel important at work or given real opportunities to control.

Rewards can be linked, as appropriate, to the various motives described earlier (or to other motives). For the maximum effect on innovative effort, they need also to be linked to innovative outcomes.

Many people introducing innovative processes in an organisation opt for a sort of 'idea scheme'. These tend to be tied to some sort of incentive base. Idea schemes, as boxes on walls which stand apart from the normal lines of communication, do seem to work − for a short time. In our experience they are temporary methods. But the negative side of them is the 'carrot', the offered incentive.

Certainly, ideas which are valuable should result in some reward, even monetary, for the individual or group who came up with it. And it's more likely to be a group. But will the organisation's members really continue to yield ideas if they see one or two earning prizes? 'Why contribute . . . save it for the idea scheme; you get paid there.'

The short answer: reward ideas. Don't offer bribes.

2. The Organisation

The innovative process is a dependent process; without a new idea, there's no process.

It is possible to describe the process in terms of the life cycle of an idea. But this is inadequate, as the life cycle is essentially an imposition of either the corporate environment (people decide what's good, bad, a priority, a delay, etc.) or the larger external environment ('a good idea, but it won't sell'). But these interactive influences establish a second feature of the process – it's dynamic. As such, it's vulnerable (you can only kill living things) and it's part of the organisation from the moment a new idea is desired.

> 'A good idea is the enemy of a better one. You stop looking for alternatives.'
>
> Tudor Rickards, Director, Creativity Programme,
> Manchester Business School, UK

Ultimately any organisation that seeks to encourage innovation must accept the fact that the innovative process cannot be separated from the on-going dynamism of the organisation. It must be part of the normal life of the organisation. If you have innovative intents, then these must be reflected in the objectives of individuals. You don't communicate for communication's sake; you communicate facts and ideas – much better they be innovative ideas than a rehash of yesterday's. As you build monitoring and control systems, should their emphasis be on the established (which are easy to monitor, they are doing as expected or are in 'exception'), or on the novel? When you plan, you don't redate last year's plan, although we've all seen it done. No, you prospect for a new future.

There is no separate innovative process for an organisation. Innovation is one of the core dynamic elements of the organisation, an element which is idea-dependent. As it is vulnerable, so is the organisation. You can kill an idea in a second; keep doing it for long enough and the organisation is similarly 'dead'.

Thus, to manage innovation it is essential to build the need and desire for innovation into the normal day-by-day activities of the organisation. This places a high level of commitment on management. They must communicate their interest in innovative ideas in such a way that their interest permeates the organisation. Difficult? Probably, but it can and is being done. Look at the successful, confident companies around you. Isn't a large part of the success of many of them founded in their preparedness to view change positively, to redirect their futures – in short, to innovate?

To repeat ourselves a little: innovations do occur accidentally. Of course, such innovations may be inadequate or irrelevant. Accidents often are. And it is not enough to wait for accidents. It is much better to be deliberately dynamic and to strive for adequate, relevant innovation. This may mean deliberately affecting the physical, group and organisational environment.

(a) PHYSICAL ENVIRONMENT

There are at least two things to consider here.

The first is the nature of 'space' for 'letting the head run'. People *do* need quiet space in which to think and reflect. Groups need space in which to work, run idea generation sessions and develop screening, evaluation and planning procedures. That same space needs to be equipped. The demands are modest: whiteboards, flipcharts, space to hang and display the thoughts, pictures, lists and decisions of the groups. Chairs and lounge areas and simple screen/overhead projector facilities, together with video replay equipment (films can be useful triggers to new approaches), complete the basic requirements. If the space and resources aren't already available, providing it is a modest investment in a better future.

The second is the nature of the daily work place. If you work in a stable, and have done so for many years, it would be difficult for you to visualise a modern office space. Similarly, an environment which is 'sterile' is unlikely to provide the stimulation you need to think. Here's a little example . . . something you can try. Go to your advertising agency. Absorb the sights and sounds. Now, go directly to your auditor's office. The environmental contrast should be obvious (and we can save a lot of words here).

(b) GROUP ENVIRONMENT

'Too many cooks spoil the broth' – perhaps, but too few means we'll have to eat the same soup day after day.

The encouragement of ideas and the search for innovative solutions require conditions that are more easily created within groups than within the mind of a single individual. Conditions such as varied sources of inputs, varied perspectives and the mutual provision of unexpected 'triggers' are basic group properties. Importantly, within groups a climate conducive to offering and acceptance of the unusual can be easily built. Further, groups can bring together a diversity of experiences, knowledge and viewpoints. Individually, we're all a little hamstrung.

Each individual in a group enters with his or her unique frame of reference, a special way of viewing the world, the opportunity or the problem. Individual perceptions differ widely. Group members quite simply offer different 'obvious' answers to open-ended problems – and what's obvious to one member may not have been obvious to anybody else.

The idea output of a group is in practice always more than the sum of the ideas of group members if taken individually and separately. Why is this so? Probably simply because groups are essentially dynamic. Interaction between individuals is stimulating. This synergistic effect gives greater chance of positive innovative outcomes from a group. One person's comment or idea triggers a second person, and this person's response triggers a third, and so on.

Idea-generation groups need not be too carefully structured if the tools described in Chapter 7 are used. Any group of individuals can be encouraged to provide ideas. We've all got a right brain. Of course, there are advantages in having one or two suspected superior divergent thinkers in the group. But beware: the rare, highly divergent thinker in a group may be less creative than you hoped in these group situations because of peer and/or normative pressures in the group. He or she may spend some time avoiding anticipated ridicule. Idea-generation groups, using any of the tools, must be open and non-judgmental; if they're not, the divergent, right-brain activity will close down, and you'll get instead careful responses designed more to 'win points' than to contribute the truly novel.

Groups often have more than merely idea-generation intents, particularly management groups. They're often involved with the total innovative processes, and may be called by a variety of names (e.g. 'Project Team', 'Study Group', 'CIP Team'). Others have partial involvement in the innovative process, but have primary roles somewhat beyond only idea-generation (e.g. 'Quality Circle' groups, 'Productivity Improvement Teams'). Others may have an 'environment search' or opportunity recognition function (e.g. Strategic Planning Group).

Where more than idea generation is involved, deliberately structured groups have a role. Such structuring means ensuring a balance of convergent and divergent skills (a Mindmix), and raises implications and difficulties for the group leader.

Let's look at a typical Mindmix group. You need:

- **Divergent thinkers** – to provide the truly different ideas during idea-generation activities, and to provide fresh approaches to strategies for improving and protecting ideas.

- **Convergent thinkers** – for analysis and evaluation of ideas, and the drawing up of implementation plans.
- **People with both skills** – to provide a 'bridge' or play an interpreter role between the convergent and divergent individuals.

MEGA-BREAKTHROUGH FROM STUPIDITY

Carver Mead, visionary physicist, Professor of Computer Science (California), on Robert Noyce's invention, in 1959, of the integrated circuit:

'It came from a very, very stupid question about something we were doing that was even more stupid'.

Business Review Weekly, April 8, 1988

In our work, we don't find it always necessary deliberately to structure groups. Frequently, the normal interdisciplinary nature of, say, project teams, ensures a range of cerebral preferences. But where we find 'bland' and/or non-productive groups, we do investigate and/or restructure via the DPA technology referred to in Chapter 2. As you may recall, the DPA measures a person's cerebral preference in quantitative (QN) *vs* qualitative (QL) terms as a percentage split. We find it useful to have some members of the group highly qualitative (say 30:70 or thereabouts), some highly quantitative (say, 70:30 or thereabouts), and some in and around the 50:50 score.

The 30:70s commonly provide a source of divergent thinking; the 70:30s commonly provide a source of convergent thinking; and the 50:50s act as sub-group leaders and 'keep the peace' by interpreting between the otherwise separated divergent and convergent sub-groups. Often, simply sharing DPA results openly within the team provides an opportunity to discuss different roles in the group and encourages an acceptance of the value of these different thinking styles.

(c) ORGANISATIONAL ENVIRONMENT

Managers involved in innovation should accept at more than the usual lip-service value, the following:

- Ideas come from people.
- The organisation is nothing but people, and its structure, the relationship of these people, can be idea-assisting (innovative), or idea-depressing (bureaucratic).
- What people call 'culture' is in effect a description of the enablers and/or constrainers to getting work done.

Let's look first at structure.

Growing economies breed bigger organisations to handle more complex tasks. And with big organisations, it's often the structure itself that gets in the way: it's the way jobs are designed and related, the reporting patterns, the way people are 'compartmentalised'. The reasons behind the growth of bureaucracies within what should be externally oriented purposeful organisations are complex. In part it's a function of size. And the bigger the organisation becomes the greater the need to clarify the structure – 'So people really know what they're supposed to be doing', of course. So the structure becomes more rigid, more procedures manuals are written, and almost without realising it another bureaucracy is born! And bureaucracy is the arch enemy of creativity and innovation.

In part, it's also a result of the use within organisations, with consequential build-up of impressive internal systems, of some academic management theories by people who have overlooked the fact that they are indeed theories, and theories need testing and usually refinement before they become usable practical tools. So the means becomes the end, and the organisation becomes constipated.

In part it's a consequence of computer technologies; the systems man, possibly convergent and potentially bureaucratic, has been elevated in status (although the advent of simpler technologies and languages may currently be providing a way out from this one).

In part, it's the natural spread of increased socialistic pressures in society; the separation of income expectation from individual contribution does not encourage individual action or idea-generation.

In part, it's a result of increased regulatory intervention; the growth of bureaucracies in the public sector has certainly spawned a generation of bureaucrats within the private sector to answer the queries of their counterparts in government departments.

And in part, it's a question of our educational processes.

Not one of these is an adequate explanation in itself, although possibly the synergism of the total may explain the growth of bureaucracy. But it could not have occurred unless management had let it. Management has been lured into accepting unnecessary bureaucracy by the presence of necessary bureaucracy. This is important; not all bureaucracy is 'bad'; the issue here is the extent of unnecessary bureaucracy and its effect on innovation. Mostly it's a negative effect.

The story on page 87 highlights the *formality* that develops in organisations. Rules, procedures, traditions, the behaviour of colleagues, all condition our heads to go down conventional paths. And we can become so conditioned to this left-brain dominated behaviour that we forget there are other ways. Take almost any medium-sized organisation (and many small ones are no different), add some formality and structure, then give it five or ten years of 'tradition'. And you've a nice, comfortable bureaucracy.

The conflict is fundamental. Bureaucracy is convergent. Objectives are preordained, our own roles are prescribed (job descriptions see to that), and efficiency measures are usually short-term input/output ratios. It's okay if the road you are travelling down has no sharp curves, no rough patches, and the world around you stays tranquil. But that kind of predictability has little to do with innovation – and innovation finds it hard to have much to do with bureaucracy.

'Management, change thyself!' is the challenge of today, and it needs to happen quickly. It is possible: the situation is not completely bleak. But change can happen only if the need for change is acknowledged by the managers themselves. It is energy focused towards the marketplace and a proper recognition of bottom-line requirements that needs very quickly to become the dominant objective of managers. We need only to overcome our own constraints to overcome the bureaucratic obstacle. We need to respect divergence; in so doing, we will automatically modify our attitudes.

Structure, by necessity, creates hierarchy which in turn presents opportunities for managers to meet power, authority and status needs; and that can be a trap for egocentric players.

Hierarchy, in organisations where it's accepted as important, stifles divergent thinking. The boss who reinforces his own ego and need for status by believing that none of his underlings' ideas could be as good as his own quickly kills divergent thinking among his people. They either quit, or accept living a strongly left-brain work life in a 'do as I say' climate.

We know of one senior manager in a large non-profit organisation who commonly refuses to accept messages telephoned through to him by the secretary of an equally senior manager in another department. Regardless of the message, he feels this is demeaning to him. His status is not being recognised. The likelihood of that view of what managing is about being conducive to divergent thinking and novel ideas is remote! Divergence is likely to be seen by that manager as a threatening attempt to rock the boat. Employees in that department with a concern for output, especially *novel* output, find themselves held back by an excessive concern for appearances and protocol. Right-brain potential shrivels in that climate.

'And God created the organisation and gave it dominion over man.'

Genesis 1, 30A subparagraph (viii)
Source: Townsend, R., *Up the Organisation*, Coronet Books, 1971

THE TOWNSEND INNOVATION TEST

Robert Townsend, one-time Chairman of Avis Rent-a-Car, and author of *Up the Organisation*, suggested how anybody could get an almost infallible reading on the value of a new idea:

1 If it receives from most people a reaction falling between active indifference and hot opposition, the idea is valid. It's worth is directly proportional to the opposition created.
2 If everyone immediately says 'terrific idea', it's probably of minor consequence. The chances are you're just telling them what they want to hear: and there's usually not much innovation in that.

Up the Organisation, Coronet Books, 1971

Similar results are seen when a manager has an excessive need for power or control. *Some* need to control is a prerequisite for successful managing – numerous studies have revealed this – but when it grows to a point where the control is through a process of elimination of novel group contribution, that is, a 'do as I say' method, then it destroys creative potential.

A senior manager once invited us to be present when he was going to seek from his management team their contributions to an important 'new business' project at their regular meeting. He started by naming a manager and asking for his ideas. Within five minutes it was clear that only those ideas coinciding with the boss's views were 'good'. Divergent offerings were met with scorn and visible irritation. Within five minutes more the meeting was reduced to a classroom parody. The senior manager was going to show them who was *really* in control here!

On organisation:

'We constantly seem to be attempting to use yesterday's organisation today to get us to tomorrow, which won't even be there when we arrive.'

Stanley Davis, Boston University

MANAGING AND MAINTAINING INNOVATION IN LARGE ORGANISATIONS

The difficulty of maintaining innovation in large organisations has been described by P. Haggerty, the President of Texas Instruments – a highly innovative firm that only recently was small but has now become very large. His experience merits extensive quotation:

'As the organisation grows, it gets more complex. Hundreds and then thousands of people are involved, often in multiple locations. The number of customers grows. Operations expand into many states and often into many countries . . . To exploit the invention or innovation fully and to get broad distribution, the price must come down. The margin between price and cost gets narrower. At a relatively early stage in the development . . . it becomes far more important that the principal managers be good administrators than that they be good innovators.

'. . . Quite understandably, we begin to get a preponderance of what, for the simplification of the concept, I will call administrative managers. They can exploit the innovation, but the skills they need and admire in themselves, in their peers, in their superiors and subordinates, are the skills of administration including leadership. Hence, the people they need and select are, in turn, predominantly administrative managers.

'. . . Often they have succeeded or displaced the original innovators and sometimes have suffered justifiable despair at the inability of the innovators to perform adequately the increasingly difficult administrative tasks. At the same time many an innovator fails to recognise how bad he really is as an administrator. His own experience and value systems simply do not qualify him to comprehend what is involved, how difficult it is to get the administrative management job done, and how justified the administrative manager is in his despair.

'As a consequence, from their own experience, the administrative managers have no basis on which to judge and respect the contribution that the innovator can really make. All they are able to see is his muddling and, too often, thoroughly inadequate ability to administer. So, they grow the organisation by accretion, adding the kind of products and service that flow naturally from the business one is already in, supplementing the markets in which one already engages, doing effective work in cutting costs and lowering prices – all essential, but unlikely to provide the step function in product and service necessary for dynamic growth.

'. . . Because they are efficient administrators, the net result is often constructive and results in the total organisation's being more effective, more profitable and more useful to society. But, at the same time, it makes the organisation still more complex and decreases the relative number of those who know how to innovate, and innovation gets increasingly harder. At some point, the growth rate slows down or falls below that of the industries in which the organisation exists.'

('The Conditions for Success in Technological Innovation'. OECD, 1971 (Paris), p. 58)

And he did. He was, he thought. What was equally clear was that divergent thoughts had no place. Acquiescence was what the boss wanted, and clear recognition of his power. So acquiescence was what he got, and conventional thinking reigned supreme. Judge for yourself the degree of commitment felt by that group to whatever actions may have been agreed to, even the conventional actions!

Now, let's look at culture.

Organisational culture can be defined as 'the way we do things around here'. The best culture for innovation is an open culture which encourages the 'ways of doing things' listed below. The primary catalyst is *you* (Mr/Ms/Miss/Mrs Manager):

- Listen to subordinates. If they're the good people they were when you recruited them, they'll have some ideas. If they've been slow to offer them, you might ask them why they feel reluctant to speak out (you'll get some more clues about culture that way, too).
- Use the idea-generation methods described later in this book. Give your people a chance to read about them, too, before putting them into practice.
- When ideas start to come, *delay* judging them. Ban the word 'No' from your initial reactions. Agree instead on some positive features of the idea. You might even want to do this formally, and make it part of your 'ideas procedures': before anybody can criticise an idea, they must first identify two positive, constructive aspects of it.
- Extend the thought above by banning 'killer phrases' from ideas meetings.
- Bring divergent thinkers, from whatever level in the hierarchy, into your idea groups. Apart from giving more and probably better ideas, this offers clear signals that status and authority have little to do with your innovatory activities at this stage.
- Be tolerant of the bizarre ideas and the wrong tracks that the group goes down occasionally. Be supportive, not critical, and tolerate the mistakes. There are sure to be some

and, if you punish mistakes made while trying, you quickly remove incentives for trying again.

- Try to understand the motives of each of the people with whom you work, and offer rewards appropriate to those motives. This is not a complex question; the greatest mechanism you have for rewarding is your tongue. Simple statements which fit the need, which provide feedback appropriate to the individual's motive profile, may be more important than complex benefit packages.
- Try to make work a more pleasant, satisfying, challenging and rewarding experience for everyone. At least some might respond with a good idea!

This might look easy. Of course, it's like hang-gliding; it's harder that it looks.

Superficially, it is all aimed at bringing about a 'culture' for innovation. Our view may be a little unusual here. We are *not* advocating that, as a primary objective, a manager should set out to create a particular 'culture'. But if a manager is getting on well with the business of generating ideas, evaluating them, and generally innovating in the ways suggested here, then before long he or she will realise that this much talked of culture has somehow caught up with them!

Culture comes primarily as a result of people doing things in certain ways together and sharing in the outcomes. Once there, of course, it becomes reinforcing and encourages more people who seek that culture to join the group and become productive, and generate further desirable outcomes, which further develops the culture – and so on.

The manager's task, therefore, is *not* to find the largest book he or she can on 'How to create a culture for innovation', and make that the first task. The task is to get on with generating ideas within the team. That's the first step down the innovation road. If it's done well, the culture you need develops. But it develops *because* things are done well, not because somebody set out to first and foremost build it.

Many factors contribute to this emerging culture. The man-

OBSTACLES

A pharmaceutical packaging line was having trouble: bottles kept breaking when being capped. The engineers adjusted the machine as finely as possible, but occasional runs of breakage still occurred. The bottle manufacurer's specifications were thoroughly checked, as well as those of the cap manufacturer. No one asked the operator of the machine, but he fixed it when he finally had freedom to do so (and that was when all the 'experts' were locked away working on the problem). He had noticed the effective part of the machine seemed dry during the breakages, so he rigged a second spot-oiler above the machine. It was only a tin from the canteen with a hole in the bottom, and it was only tied in place somewhat tentatively, but it worked.

This story highlights the *formality* that develops in organisations. Rules, procedures, traditions, the behaviour of colleagues, all condition our heads to go down the convergent path . . . the trusted and comfortable analytical route. And, of course, we may just miss the excellent intuitive, albeit informal, answer.

---

ager's own behaviour will be one important determinant. A manager can send out powerful signals by keeping his or her behaviour in line with stated preferences. Example is a powerful communicative device!

If managers want a culture supportive of innovation they must be seen to want it, and they (and their closest aides) must communicate this within the organisation. In surveys with which we've been associated in organisations in which the top management has expressed innovative growth objectives, it is frequently seen that the lower echelons:

- Considered management somewhat blind to external events, particularly threats.
- Considered that maintenance of the status quo was a deliberate organisational objective.
- Felt management did not make use of the talent and data already available in the organisation.

(We have taken some liberty to summarise the types of responses, with subsequent language modification. But the meaning's not changed.) Perhaps top management simply forgot to tell them, or perhaps saying something is not as powerful as doing!

We've used the following analogy before, but it's worth repeating in this different context. Ideas generated within an organisation are like seeds in the garden; they need careful nurturing, the surrounds must be constantly weeded, the young plants may require support, etc., before the fruit can be gathered. The gardening group must contain an enthusiast to keep the idea going when things are tough, an agronomist to solve problems with his technical knowledge, and someone in authority (a patron or sponsor) to make sure resources are available. The successful cropping and movement of the fruit to users requires entrepreneurial skills.

This analogy somewhat takes to task the common hierarchical structure of organisations. But we do have available knowledge of human behaviour, individually and organisationally, to permit structural relationships more likely to lead to innovation than to bureaucracy. It is possible, for example, to measure potential entrepreneurial skill. The data may be somewhat less than complete, but it's certainly better than relying on the 'he'll fit in' criterion. We can measure accurately quantitative and qualitative preferences, and we can measure the demands and opportunities for these accurately in jobs. This is the DPA technology mentioned in Chapter 2 and elsewhere; it can give 'good fit'! Also, alternate models to the 'organisational chart' are available. The organisation can be viewed as a dynamic phenomenon, as a molecule, with specific 'org-atoms' performing tasks both functionally (e.g. accounting, marketing of in-line products) or future-oriented (e.g. R & D). And functional 'org-atoms' as dynamic entities are every bit as potentially innovative as their future-oriented cousins. (This alternative model is expanded as selective reading at the end of this Chapter. Don't use your time on it unless it interests you. See page 100).

A MANAGEMENT STYLE FOR INNOVATION?

A recent study of 165 effective, entrepreneurial managers (spread over five companies) indicated that the managers achieved success by:

- Persuading rather than ordering their people around. Real pressure was used only as a last resort.
- Building teams. That meant frequent meetings, and a good deal of sharing of information.
- Gaining ideas from others – from peers – from subordinates – and welcoming their comments, critical as well as supportive.
- Acknowledging what others had at stake in the project – being aware of their needs, and organisational politics.
- Giving recognition willingly, when it was due, and sharing rewards willing.

(R. Moss Kanter, 'The Middle Manager as Innovator',
Harvard Business Review, July–August 1982)

---

3. The Process

As managers you may often feel swamped by the variety of supposedly new techniques available to you. Some of the more common processes are related to Mindmix in later chapters, but it's worth looking briefly at this relationship here – that is, what parts of those processes are better serviced by right-brain, divergent, qualitative persons and what parts are better serviced by left-brain, convergent, quantitative persons. Part of your challenge is to bring these seemingly disparate individuals together to capitalise on their differential strengths, and to increase your chance of managing the 'whole' brain.

Organisations already use a wide variety of management processes, and it's important to see how Mindmix relates to some of the major ones. Take for example the SWOT analysis (Strengths and Weaknesses, Opportunities and Threats) often used early in the process of corporate planning. Most managers would approach this in an analytic, left-brain fashion. After all, the organisation has long regarded analytic skills as 'good', has been suspicious of intuition, especially at middle management and lower levels, and is well aware of the use of the word 'analysis' in the very label used for the SWOT technique. But look at what SWOT requires: company Strengths – are these all identifiable by convergent means? And Weakness? Some imaginative interpretations would seem to have a part to play here, as well as traditional analytic or convergent thinking. A review of the external environment, in terms of Opportunities or Threats, is likely to offer an even greater chance for productive, divergent thinking. Some of the most valued opportunities will be those not seen by your left-brain dominated competitors, like:

- **Visine, Pfizer eye-drop product:** Pfizer saw the opportunity in the market place for 'cosmetic' use for eye drops,

and promoted Visine with the theme 'take the red out'. People who wanted to have better-looking eyes made Visine market leader.

- **The VW Kombi:** an unusual square box on wheels. Volkswagen saw an opportunity there over thirty years ago, which competitors largely disregarded until fairly recently.
- **Kiwi fruit:** an improved and renamed Chinese gooseberry, now sold in volume internationally since a creative examination of the market revealed the opportunity.
- And the **T-model Ford**, the **ballpoint pen**, etc.

This same need to *add* some divergent thinking exists in subsequent stages of planning, regardless of the particular planning label used (corporate, business, strategic, operational, etc).

How else can you find that desirable strategy which will differentiate your future from the future of the 'also rans'? (See Chapter 5.)

Our experience with formal, postgraduate management education indicates that most practising managers (the 'students' at postgraduate level) have difficulty in adding divergent thinking to their planning approaches. After their two, three or four years of left-brain education, and repeated insistence on building analytical skills, that's hardly surprising. But it leaves their responses to broad policy and planning issues relatively impoverished, at least in the early days of their exposure.

It reflects, sadly, the common belief that planning is 'better' when it's highly rational. That may reflect people's discomfort with uncertainty, which is understandable, especially if the planning is concerned with high value and/or important outcomes. But the solution is not to create an artificial sense of security by staying within the known confines of convergent planning techniques. That way the real opportunities, the breakthrough visions of a new way ahead into our tomorrows, are likely not to be found. The jump from where we are now, into those new visions of where we want to be, is not a jump that can be made with a purely convergent approach. Right-brain divergence needs to be added so that the novel, the unexpected, the unanticipated, the new, can be mixed with the offerings from the conventional analyses. Some managers intuitively know that this is how it has to be. For others, who are suspicious of the value of right-brain thinking, the first need is to establish a sense of legitimacy for divergent approaches. This book may help do that.

These comments apply broadly to other functions in organisations in addition to planning. There are R & D groups, marketing groups, market researchers, operations and production groups, to name just a few. All have needs, at different times, to incorporate divergent thinking into their work day. It will not be needed in *every* day's work perhaps. But better problem-solving of open-ended issues requires divergence. In conventional language, it is the 'alternatives generation' stage of problem-solving. Regardless of what it's called, the need for divergence is there.

At the level of the individual, problem solving is mostly a sequential process of convergent/divergent/convergent phases. In a group setting, however, both cerebral processes can be operating simultaneously, although in separate heads. Individual head A can be running down a convergent ideas track, and at the same time individual head B can be operating divergently. This combination is Mindmix at work.

The manager's challenge is to win acceptance of the value of right-brain contributions, and then to establish opportunities for both right and left brains to be engaged in seeking opportunities and solving problems.

The target over time is always the same. Develop the capacity and ability for a whole brain approach.

Consider your own organisation, and others you have local knowledge of. You've seen good ideas die for want of a supportive attitude. We've seen them by the hundreds. Often their deaths are hardly noticed. There are no funerals, no rituals, to cause us to reflect on the lives of ideas. It's more often a case of 'whatever happened to . . .', and 'well, it just faded away'. Good ideas don't just fade away. They're slaughtered by rampaging squads of carefully attired, analytical managers.

As the top of an organisation requests and encourages ideas, the bottom responds. Why not? Here are the numbers and the diversity to provide ideas . . . and often, here are the truly divergent. So, there's an increased flow of ideas upwards. This can be uncomfortable for the middle. Here sit the carefully selected 'good analysts', the convergent experts, the experts at rejecting the unusual. (All that is, of course, a little unfair – they're probably only the consequence of their education, and they're probably only hiding their own natural divergence.) In many organisations, there are good reasons for middle management to opt for the safe path, to avoid notoriety, not to 'rock the boat', and to find perfectly valid reasons for saying 'no' to imperfectly formed ideas.

This means, of course, that an increase of idea-flow upwards can increase the flow downwards of the word 'No'. Which won't help employee relationships one little bit. Not only will the middle management feel alienated ('their idea scheme!') but the lower level employees will feel frustrated ('not any good talking to them; they won't listen!').

We can illustrate this problem, and the answer, diagrammatically:

(a) Without attention to the risk of middle management alienation:

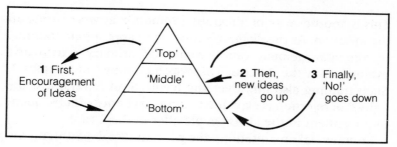

The way around is fully to involve middle management in the innovative process. Make them the experts at evaluation, for example. Give them control of evaluative criteria, so they can feed back *reasons* for 'no', as well as some 'yesses' when appropriate. Perhaps they'll get triggered into requesting more information, or more ideas. Certainly, they'll find opportunities to be 'heroes' by backing the good ones, and sending them up above for futher investigation, approval, or whatever.

Of course, if you accept this argument (and you should; it's rather obvious), then acknowledge that middle managers need a good understanding of the entire idea-generation – idea-evaluation – ideas-improvement/protection model. They need to know where they fit. And they need to be *good* evaluators.

(b) With deliberate use of middle managers as primary screen and evaluation:

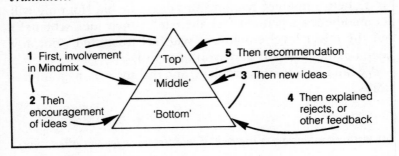

This is another way of illustrating Mindmix at work inside an organisation. As the diagram shows, with appropriate training, middle management can become the primary screen and evaluation in the process. This was mentioned in Chapter 3. Such training also improves the feedback of rejection. If the 'why?' of rejection is explained, there's a chance of subsequent improvement in the ideas people offer in the future.

Commercial organisations and government departments are not usually hotbeds of innovation. Novel ideas, original approaches to problems, creative solutions are often said to be important, often said to be the way into our future, often said to be the pathway to organisational excellence – but in practice something gets in the way. The lip service paid to innovation is seen, at the end of the day, to be mostly just lip service.

HOW WELL ARE WE DOING?

At this point it may be useful to take a look at how well your organisation, or your section or department, is doing in this business of innovating.

First, what percentage of sales comes now from products or services that we were not selling at all

(a) 5 years ago?   Answer (a) _____ per cent
(b) 10 years ago?   Answer (b) _____ per cent

This will provide a rough guide to the level of dependency on innovative activity. It's also useful to identify the sources of the ideas, the key people who made the various innovations happen, and the extent to which the changes were deliberate rather than fortuitous. Identifying why some ideas are winners and why others weren't can also be instructive.

Next, what percentage of sales from existing products or services are we likely to lose over the next five years? (Keep product life-cycle concepts in mind here.)

Answer: at least _____ per cent; at most _____ per cent

Now repeat the questions, substituting 'profit' for 'sales'.

If it's difficult to get hold of the information you need in order to answer these questions, then you have identified an area where some innovation is probably essential. That's the 'management information systems' area. You're now in a position to guestimate how likely it is that your existing plans for innovatory effort will successfully bridge this gap between where you are today and where you'd like to be tomorrow.

So, how likely? Tick the box.

☐ Very likely we will be okay at our present level of effort.
☐ We might just be okay at our present level of effort.
☐ It's unlikely we'll be okay.

If you've ticked any box other than the first one, you're probably looking at an innovation gap. You could try and get around it by a strategy of acquisition, mergers, or licensing in know-how or products that you require. Some organisations go this way. Others can't, for a variety of reasons, or they simply believe that an adequate level of internally generated innovation is a basic requirement for long-term organisational health. But given a 'gap' and a belief that it should be closed at least in part by internal innovation/development activity, then your organisation is facing a real need to plan and innovate its way into a successful future. If at this stage you sit still, you begin to look more and more like one of those dinosaurs.

If you think some more positive action would be sensible – read on.

AN ALTERNATIVE VIEW OF THE ORGANISATION

Organisations can be viewed as atom-like and molecular-like. This view can help overcome some of the bureaucratic and control approaches to describing organisations, and thus assist towards the innovative organisation.

The basic building block of matter is the atom. It has a nucleus, which might be described as a somewhat 'heavy' centre, around which move much lighter and more active electrons. Within any organisation, atom-like relationships are everywhere; the supervisor or manager is a nucleus for his or her work group; they are as electrons in their relationship to him. Or the executive committee has a group of highly charged managers who 'buzz' around it – again, an atom-like structure. These org-atoms (to use a convenient term) are the basic building blocks of organisations.

Any individual may obviously be a member of more than one org-atom, depending on which particular viewpoint is taken. Further, his or her role may be different from org-atom to org-atom. For example, a sales manager may clearly be the nucleus (or part of the nucleus) of the sales group, but may be an inner-electron of the marketing group.

Within the atom, the nucleus may be made up simply of one proton (a positively charged particle); this is the case with a hydrogen atom. Other elements have a greater number of protons, and also additional neutrons (uncharged particles). The nuclei of the org-atom structures in organisations are similarly sometimes an individual, and sometimes a group. In the atom, the neutrons have a positive role; they provide stability to the nucleus. Similarly, in org-atoms it is not unusual that there exists within a central management group one or more persons who are not true decision-makers.

Large org-atoms with heavy nuclei tend to attract large numbers of neutrons – and tend to need them! If they grow too large, it doesn't matter how many neutrons are added, they simply break down as they are intrinsically unstable – and thus, for example, divisions are formed. You can no doubt think of neutron-like individuals in your organisation. They work! They keep the competing elements together.

Within the atom, electrons do the work – they are involved in bridging, transmission of energy and the protection of the nucleus. It takes a major force to upset or activate the nucleus, but little effort to stimulate the electrons. Similarly in an org-atom, the boss (or nucleus) is normally a relatively dormant centre. His role is to use the energies of the electrons.

It doesn't take much effort to see how the model can be used to help subordinate managers see their role more clearly. A simple sketching of this analogy, in particular the relatively dormant role of the nucleus but the usefulness of the electrons outside it, can provide lessons on delegation, the nature of communications, the value of positive feedback, etc.

5
Innovation and Strategic Planning

Moving Inevitably to X

Innovation and Strategic Planning

Frank Herbert is a highly successful science fiction writer. His **Dune** *series has been made into a successful film. In a novel* **Whipping Star**, *Herbert's hero McKie is in conversation with a powerful non-human entity known as Fanny Mae. Fanny Mae is a 'Calebon', a fictitious star creature.*

'Fanny Mae,' he said, 'I understand you could not prevent the attack. I don't blame you. I understand.'

'Surprise connectives,' the Caledon said. 'You overstand.'

'I understand.'

Fanny Mae goes on to differentiate mere 'understanding' from 'overstanding'.

Herbert's invention of 'overstand' provides a novel viewpoint of strategic planning. While it is necessary to *understand* our here-and-now in management, it's equally necessary to *overstand* to see beyond the here and now. *Understanding* is probably a necessary condition for *overstanding* . . . Herbert doesn't make this clear, but in terms of managing forward certainly a sound knowledge of where you are at present (understanding) is essential to mapping some future location or direction (over-standing).

Now, by using Herbert as a reference, we're not trying to suggest that strategic planning is science fiction. No doubt, some of it is. But much valid planning is done in the strategic dimension.

Surveying of futures and in some way mapping strategic direction through these is an obviously essential management task. This is clearly 'overstanding', and it is difficult to see this as a convergent process, although some so-called 'strategic planning' is disappointingly convergent.

What's Strategic Planning?

Strategic planning is a dynamic and issue-oriented process to help the organisation take control of significant potential futures.

Strategic planning is more than merely long-range planning. Certainly, long-range planning can be strategic, and all strategic planning is long-range. Here's an analogy: a ship at sea can project from its bearing, the wind and current pressures, and its own generated way, where it will be at 4.00 pm tomorrow with a great deal of accuracy. That's a projective plan, and a long-range plan. Alternatively, the captain of the ship can sit down, decide where he'd like to be at 4.00 pm tomorrow, and then work out how he can get there (perhaps by lightening the ship, or by other innovative strategies). That's a *strategic plan*. It's also a long-range plan. ('Tomorrow' is a concept here, not a date).

Strategic planning is also business planning. Of course, it's not the immediate business plan (i.e. the annual budget), but it does affect it. The annual budget/business plan will include activities relating to strategies or parts of strategies from the strategic plan of relevance to the planning period.

The relationship can be show as:

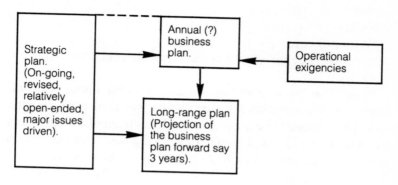

The outcomes of such planning are strategies identified and accepted as appropriate to the overall goal. Action plans can be built for and about each of these strategies.

There is a variety of planning models which purport to be 'strategic'. Many are simply projective, some merely statistical (quantitative). Such are necessarily convergent. But if we are to come up with *novel* outcomes, strategies which by their potential significance demand a place in the future, the need for divergent thinking is clear. Tomorrows which are only a projection of today suggest at the best maintenance strategies; tomorrows which are different from today (but built on the base of today) suggest divergent input into the planning process.

But our plan's important . . .?

At a recent meeting, the CEO of a large corporation was explaining problems of planning. He was questioned on the Planning base: 'Do you have a "vision" or "mission" statement?'

'Certainly,' came the reply, 'it's at the front of our Strategic Plan'.

'May we see it?' we asked.

'Well . . . the plan's very important. It's acutally confidential.'

'Who has copies?'

'Only the key people involved,' was the reply.

Here's the catch! How do you get desirable divergent challenge into your planning if there's no opportunity for the plan
to be questioned? The answer's simple: you don't. The problem
lies with methods employed in developing the strategic plan. In
the example above, they were clearly as secretive as the status
of the finished plan. (And this ignores the question of how do
you implement and get commitment to a secret plan?)

The problems of planning our CEO was experiencing were
clearly the consequence of an attitude to strategic planning. 'It's
so important it has to be confidential.' Try this one day . . . to
increase the readership of trivia, stamp it confidential. It's
importance is instantly elevated, and it's in demand!

To ensure divergent input into the planning process, it is
necessary to break through this attitude, to clearly separate
importance from confidentiality, to see them as independent
phenomena. And this can be done by modification of the
method of preparation of the strategic plan.

ICI openly acknowledge the need for divergent inputs. Alan
Hayes, Group chief planner (UK) at the time, says of the 'old'
approach of the 1960's and early 1970's:

> '. . . planning was a very numerate activity . . . that was the
> era which produced planning as a profession – slide rules,
> critical path diagrams, and all the rest of it. The General
> Manager, Planning, used competitive ratios to point out what
> they should be thinking about . . . All of which was perhaps
> appropriate to an era of growth.'

But it was inappropriate to the new world into which ICI has
moved, so that left-brain dominant planning approach is now
much less prominent. What's important today – factors like

quality or research, and marketing effort – are less easily quantified. 'You see,' says Hayes, 'it has become more and more a question of judgment. Business deals are done from the guts: that's how people make millions'.[1]

ICI have, in the language of Mindmix, added a great deal of divergent thinking to their planning processes.

THE SAME SENTIMENTS IN AUSTRALIA – BRINGING INTUITION INTO PLANNING

'Strategic planning requires the application of not only analytical, deductive problem-solving skills but also the inductive skills required for creative thinking and the good old-fashioned gut-feel.'

John Cardon, Director, Finance, CRA Ltd
(*Business Review Weekly*, 15–21 October 1983)

GE's Major Appliance Business Group says the same thing. Planners, then separate from line managers '. . . were usually right, but they were frequently wrong – usually because they relied on data, not market instincts, to make their judgments,' says Roger Schipke, chief executive.[2]

Planning Process

The commonly applied process of planning towards future strategies is summarised in the diagram over the page.

Of course, much of this is commonly performed under different labels (e.g. environmental scanning as a form of analysis) and with different levels of 'overstanding'.

The critical message for effective managers/planners is the involvement of people (employees, staff) in as much of the process as possible. Only such involvement can provide divergent input.

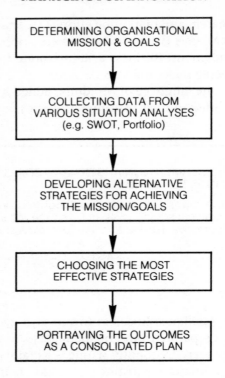

The 'how?' of this involvement requires us first to recognise the various elements in the process. These are illustrated on a schematic (on page 108), and are described below:

The mission/vision . . . the concept of what business you're in, and why you're in it, and is it what you want to be in in the future. It's essentially 'What are we?' and 'Why are we?' and 'What do we want to be?' questions.

The SWOT Analysis . . . the recognition of the strengths and weaknesses of the organisation, and of the opportunities and threats in the external environment of relevance to the mission. It's essentially a 'Where are we?' question.

The portfolio analysis . . . the recognition of issues of relevance to products, or business subdivisions. While usually a here-and-now process, it can be a projected process. It measures products or business subdivisions (in fact, any key business unit) on the basis of market attractiveness and relative competitive situation. It's essentially a 'What have we?' question.

The organisation analysis ... is another 'What have we?' question, but specifically of the organisational structure and factors which affect the human resources of this structure.

Strategic issues ... the sorting of a list from matching the SWOT, portfolio and organisation analyses against the mission. (A special note here: while the mission or vision of an organisation tends to be relatively permanent, it is foolish to view this as carved in stone. Clearly, significant opportunities, recognised by analyses, may cause a rethink of the mission. So they're shown on the schematic with interaction between the elements.) The list will have a preliminary sense of priority, or relative importance ... but this is probably not very binding at this stage.

Criteria setting ... for each recognised strategic issue, there is a need for particular resource and result measures (criteria) to permit various potential strategies to be evaluated. It is possible the same criteria may be applied to all issues, but just as logical for them to be different for each issue addressed. Of course, they're all directly influenced by the mission (which probably includes broad goal concepts), and all indirectly affected by the preliminary analyses. In particular, resource criteria need monitoring/comparison across the range of issues ... an organisation may not be able to afford to address some issues 'cheaply' because others are seen to be more important.

Idea generation (strategy possibilities) ... the generation of particular strategic concepts, or potential strategies. This is an area where divergent thoughts are clearly needed. Obviously, this process is repeated for each strategic issue.

Evaluation/reduction ... the evaluation of the potential strategies against the agreed criteria for each strategic issue. This need not be highly quantitative decision-making, but sufficient data should be gathered to permit the realistic evaluation and reduction to a manageable number of strategies for each issue. However, having refined strategies is *not* the point at this stage.

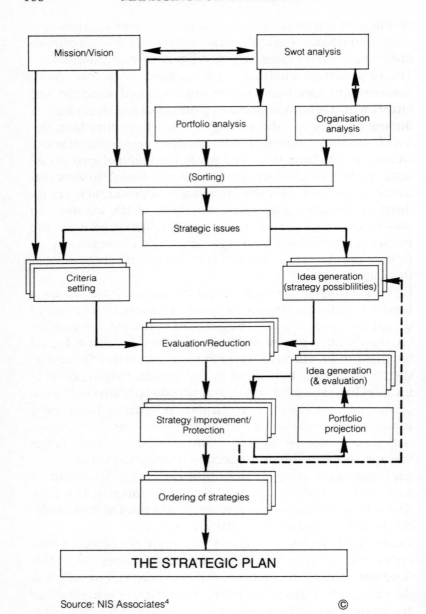

Source: NIS Associates[4]   ©

Strategy improvement/protection . . . refining the short-listed strategies, and turning each of these into plans of action. A logic for surveying of futures is essential here, and this can be supported by **portfolio projection** (to estimate the impact of changes on future market attractiveness and possible competitive changes) and further **idea generation and evaluation** to locate detailed actions to overcome the 'What might go wrong?' answers both for protection and in a contingent sense. Where unsatisfactory futures for all evaluated strategies are estimated, it may be necessary to find other possible strategies. (This is shown on the schematic by a broken line return to the Idea generation–Strategy possibilities).

Innovation: Simply a good new idea acted upon. It can come from skunk-works or champions, from associates or customers, from assembly lines or loading docks, from reception desks or boardrooms.

Brochure on Seminar 'Implementing *In Search of Excellence*', 1985

Ordering of strategies . . . setting of true priorities is now possible, *and* necessary. The earlier concept of priorities, which were deliberately loose, will possibly have changed in response to recognised strategies; some may be better than anticipated while for some issues viable strategies may have been difficult to generate. Also, the strategies usually need scheduling; it is impossible to do everything at once.

The strategic plan . . . not only the documentation of all from the Ordering, but also ensuring the feeding-in of strategies to other 'business planning' (e.g. the budgeting process).

The *disciplined* progression through these steps is the process we call strategic planning.

The Planning Method . . . Involvement

Involvement not only provides potentially desirable divergent input; it minimises problems of communication and commit-

Knowing where you want to be is important. But knowing how to get there is critical. Accessibility is part of the concept of destination.

Elements of strategic planning process	Involvement concept
1. DETERMINING THE MISSION/VISION ★	Visions are *seen*. They are right-brain imagery. The CEO who believes this is best done by self, or by the key executives (probably convergent survivors), misunderstands the value of divergent input. A group of employees, inclusive of divergent 'kinds', can throw up surprising variations of mission and vision. (Certainly, the CEO or the Board should retain the right to state this, but they'd be smart to get this input.)
2. SWOT ANALYSIS ★	SWOT is Strengths/Weaknesses/Opportunities/Threats. The value of divergent thinking in recognition of opportunities or threats is obvious. Group up the employees . . . they *see* opportunities and threats executives clearly miss.
3. ORGANISATION ANALYSIS	By process, a collation of opinions, not a question of desirable divergent, but of necessary involvement.
4. PORTFOLIO ANALYSIS	The process of placing key business units in a comparative matrix (often called 'The Boston model') is widespread in strategic planning in practice, and is essentially a convergent process. Each dimension on the matrix is in effect a single decision (see Chapter 8), one to do with market attractiveness and one to do with competitive situation. But while the matrix is essentially the consequence of convergent thinking, there's potential for divergence in recognising what are the key business units. Viewing the operational components of an organisation in a novel way, subdividing the business into previously unrecognised units, can lead to planning breakthrough. At least, we should listen to the divergent input.

5. STRATEGIC ISSUES (SORTING)	This is necessarily a 'whole brain' process, and thus a synergistic group (refer back to Chapter 3) should be helpful.
6. CRITERIA SETTING	Chapter 8 will make this clearer. Setting of criteria is essentially a convergent task. But groups tend to do it better than any one individual.
7. IDEA GENERATION (STRATEGY POSSIBILITIES) ★	Chapters 6 and 7 expand on processes useful here. Clearly divergence and groups are imperative if there's to be a range of useful, novel ideas.
8. EVALUATION/ REDUCTION (STRATEGY CHOICE)	Essentially decision-making. (See Chapter 8.)
9. STRATEGY IMPROVEMENT/ PROTECTION ★	This is a 'whole team' process similar to the logic of Idea protection/Improvement outlined in Chapter 8. There is a need here for novel ideas to improve and protect strategies, and thus for divergent input.
10. ORDERING OF STRATEGIES	Essentially a convergent task requiring quantitative skills.
11. ENVIRON- MENTAL SCANNING ★	Scanning is a sort of 'futurism'. In shorter time frames (say three years), often there is quantitative (projected) data available. But many planners, including the authors, would prefer some qualitative input as to possible futures. This is often gained via a modified Delphi Technique (see further reading). To make such 'futurism' effective, and to ensure the Delphi works, it's essential to include divergent thinkers in the groups or in the Delphic rounds.

'It is not enough to have a good mind. The main thing is to use it well.'

René Descartes

ment, thus minimising difficulties of implementation. 'Strategy implementation' has emerged as a buzz-word in management. Its very emergence is indicative of the dimension of the problem. Plans are written which sit on shelves. Why? Often the answer can be found in the extent and breadth of involvement in the planning process.

There seem to be few, if any, elements of the planning where involvement is impractical. Certainly, it's an experience that is not only possible at all steps, but desirable. The table on pp. 110–11 outlines this involvement, and the elements where divergent input, from groups, is important are marked with an asterisk.

Divergence from a Convergent Base

One way in which many planners look at the input of future changes is via portfolio analysis.

Portfolio analysis is essentially a quantitative process, providing normally a convergent map of the here-and-now. It produces a matrix, usually presented something like:

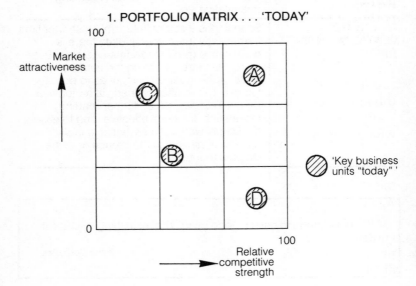

1. PORTFOLIO MATRIX . . . 'TODAY'

Conclusions are drawn from this, usually with some established colloquialisms, as to desirable strategies. For example:

- Key Business A is usually call a *star*, and strategies to maintain this position, often by increased resource allocation, are normally looked for.
- Key Business Unit D is usually called a *cash cow*, and strategies to 'milk' are usually looked for.
- Key Business Unit C is usually unnamed, but referred to as a '?', as the traditional wisdom is that this is a high-risk position for improvement strategies. The '?' indicates the real need . . . novel strategies (from divergent heads).
- Key Business Unit B, or others which might be more towards the 0 point, are usually called *dogs* and the traditional wisdom is that tactical responses are required and in extreme cases, termination.

The traditional wisdom approaches can clearly be questioned, particularly with some divergent input. For example, why not convert 'dogs' to 'cash cows'? But a more direct relationship of portfolio analysis to divergent thinking is available – projected portfolio analysis.

This can be used in two ways, both requiring posing of open-ended questions requiring divergent thinking. These are:

(i)   To answer the question 'If we do nothing, what would this key business unit be like in three (five, or whatever) years?'

(ii)   To answer the question 'If we proceed with Strategy X, what is the impact on each of the key business units?'

Referring to the previous matrix, answers to question (i) might yield matrix 2 overleaf:

Again, answers to question (ii) might yield 3 overleaf:

The potential for finding *important* but unusual answers is enormous, and clearly the structure can provide a communications link for the convergent manager to utilise the divergent input.

2. PORTFOLIO MATRIX . . . 'TOMORROW (say five years), if no strategic actions'

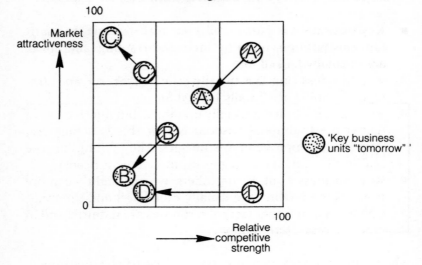

Market attractiveness

100

0

100

Relative competitive strength

'Key business units "tomorrow" '

3. PORTFOLIO MATRIX . . . 'TOMORROW (say five years), if Strategy X and Strategy Y are implemented'.

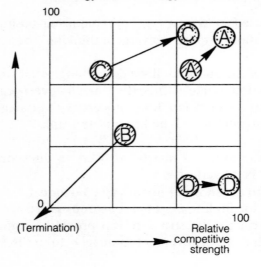

100

0

(Termination)

100

Relative competitive strength

- **A primary conclusion**: in all approaches to strategic planning, divergent input is not only desirable; it's essential if we are to create tomorrows *different* from today.
- **A secondary conclusion**: perhaps all tramps on park benches have 'overstanding' (or is 'overstanding' present in your planning people?)

A pharmaceutical company had excess capacity on a blister-packing machine. A group was posed the question 'How to utilise the blister-packing machine more efficiently?' Slip-writing was used to trigger brainstorming. One idea which emerged was for a unique wash system (and pack) for contact lenses.

Sometimes a 'good idea' is very distant from the posed problem.

Part 2

MINDMIX

Processes

6
Creative Tools for Individuals

Making Ideas Xpand

Developing a Creative Viewpoint

A creative viewpoint is a way of looking at things, a sort of fresh approach. An individual who looks around starts to see ideas everywhere – in places, people, objects and events.

It's possible to think of the world in which we live as an 'idea museum'.[1] There's the car we drive, the light switch, the pen we write with. When we trace any of these back far enough, we find they originally started in the mind of one person. Someone had an idea, and someone acted on it.

Strolling through the 'idea museum' puts us in direct contact with the history of ingenuity. These are necessarily ideas that worked, or they wouldn't be in the museum. And it can be very encouraging to realise that the biggest ideas started in small, humble ways.

At any time, a person can ask, 'I wonder where this object came from?' Some may have come from sophisticated R & D departments, but such departments can't amount to much until someone comes up with a good idea to trigger the R & D and associated planning.

Learn to be more curious; learn to ask questions continuously. 'How was this thing made?' 'Who had the idea first?', 'Why is it this shape?' can trigger new ideas. Often, one is forced to read books and articles to find the answers. And the more ideas one sees, the greater the likelihood that a new combination or extension will occur.

> 'We are all continually faced with a series of enormous opportunities, brilliantly disguised as insoluble problems.'

Ideas surface at peculiar times; when we're showering, vacuuming, playing tennis or washing the car. An example is the engineer who was looking for a solution to brake drag on Boeing 727 landing wheels. His breakthrough came while he was sweeping the front porch. He noticed the washer-type device used to keep the screen door open. In thinking about how it worked, he found the solution to his brake drag problem.

> Looking at the same thing as everyone else and seeing something different could be an ocular deficiency, but might be a creative viewpoint.

The creative viewpoint means a willingness to see ideas everywhere. For those ideas to develop and grow, however, they must be given a little time. Judging ideas prematurely is a surefire way to kill them off as well as to lose future contributions from the persons who offered them. Even if it's yourself. Evaluation of ideas is obviously necessary, but not at the time they first surface. The golden rules are:

- Suspend judgment.
- Delay evaluation, and give the new idea a chance to grow.

Idea screening and evaluation come later.

YOU'RE NEVER TOO OLD OR TOO YOUNG!

Much data suggests that the age band 30–40 years sees the greatest flow of creative achievements.

But don't forget Mozart produced minuets at five and Paul Morphy was a chess champion at twelve. Bizet, Robert Burns, Samuel Colt, Galileo, Mendelssohn, Milton, Pascal, Pope and Schubert all made notable achievements during their teens.

Bellini was writing great music for ten years *after* his 75th birthday. Cervantes wrote the second part of Don Quixote at 68, and Galileo was productive into his seventies. Thomas Hardy, Laplace, Tennyson and Verdi all continued to create at least into their seventies, and Picasso produced copiously into his nineties.

(Reitz, H. J., *Behaviour in Organisations*, Irwin, 1981)

Creative Tools for Generating Ideas

Generating novel ideas requires that we challenge the traditional, logical patterns of thinking so familiar to our left-brain dominant heads. While the convergent approach is fine, indeed necessary, for closed-ended problems, a more open, divergent or right-brain approach will be more productive with open-ended problems. This section offers some techniques for bringing more of your right-brain, divergent skills into operation.

Although working in groups is usually more productive of ideas, a group setting is not always possible. So these are methods that can be used when you are working alone. The 'principles' underlying them, however, are equally valid in the group activities and techniques described in Chapter 7.

Creativity is for everybody. The 'sale' sign on the window of a camping equipment store read:
'NOW IS THE DISCOUNT OF
OUR WINTER TENTS'

---

1. REDEFINITIONAL TECHNIQUES

Often looking at a problem or opportunity from a new perspective changes the range of ideas that present. Looking at an underused carpark as a problem of maximising usage might lead to some interesting ideas for attracting cars. Looking at it as a piece of real estate might result in a multi-storey building in which cars play a minor part.

Here are some approaches to redefining the problem:

(a) Ask all around it

One way of examining a problem for redefinition is outlined in the box on page 123. It is adapted from an approach described by Tudor Rickards, a British worker in creativity.[2]

This redefinitional technique may lead to novel approaches, or may simply lead to a more useful clarification of the original problem to which other idea-generation tools can be applied.

(b) Challenge the problem boundaries

The very act of defining a problem puts boundaries on it. Often, because these are written down, they are accepted as unchangeable.

Try breaking down the supposed boundaries by examining each element for its hidden assumptions. Often these assumptions need to be questioned to arrive at a more accurate description.

For instance, look at the problem defined here:

'How to _extend_ Amsterdam's <u>tramway system</u> to encourage <u>peak-hour car drivers</u> to use their vehicles less, and <u>public transport</u> more.'

The underlined words can be questioned. Why <u>extend</u>? Why not leave as is, but work on improving timetabling? Why not contract to provide a better inner-city service where vehicle congestion is worst?

Describe the problem for which you need some 'action' answers. Keep it brief, and keep it open-ended.

_____

_____

Now work through what follows.

(i)   The reason this problem is important is _____

_____

_____

(ii)   Problems usually have several perspectives. An alternative view of this problem is _____

_____

_____

(iii) If I had a magic wand to use on this problem, I would wish for_____

_____

_____

(iv)   The real essence of this problem is _____

_____

_____

(v)   A bizarre way of thinking about this problem is to view it as _

_____

_____

Go back now to the problem definition at the top of the page. Can you describe it in a different and more useful way?

Why the <u>tramway system</u>? Why not buses? Why not carparks at railway stations to improve train use?

Why just <u>peak-hour drivers</u>? Why not non-peak drivers, as the trams are vastly under-used in off-peak hours?

And so on. Working through these factors one by one, changing some, confirming others, may produce a more insightful and valuable definition of the problem . . . and may throw out a novel answer.

'There is nothing more important than an idea in the mind of man.'
Edward de Bono, Preface to *Eureka! All Illustrated History of Inventions* (Ed. de Bono), Holt, Rinehart & Winston, 1979

(c) Worry it with WHY?

This is a simple technique for redefining the problem based on asking questions. Simply forcing the problem or situation with the question 'Why?' may lead to a different range of ideas.

Take an example:

Problem: To catalogue the business journals coming into the department.

Why? So that their circulation can be better controlled.

Why? So that all managers have an equal chance to receive and read them.

Why? So that our people can keep themselves better informed.

Why? So that departmental effectiveness can be maintained or improved.

And so on . . . Even after just four 'Why's?' it is apparent that the *real* issue (seemingly departmental effectiveness) will need more than just cataloguing of journals if progress is to be made.

Carrying on asking 'why?' leads to yet more broadening of the problem by raising the underlying issues. Just where we choose to attack 'the problem' is our decision based on priorities and resources available. By progressively moving back from the original, *apparent* problem, we have identified more fundamental problems, solutions to any of which might make it unnecessary to answer the original one. Or might throw out a novel solution: for example, no business journals as an answer to cataloguing business journals.

Ideas even grow on trees . . .

- Alessandro Volta invented the electric battery (about 1799). He was actually trying to explain why dissected frogs' legs twitched when touched with certain metals.
- Alexander Graham Bell was actually working to design a hearing aid in 1876 when he invented the telephone.
- Rene Laence invented the stethoscope in the early nineteenth century. He got the idea from watching children at play using wooden boards to hear pins striking the far end of the boards.
- Christopher Shales didn't know he'd invented the typewriter (1870s). He had produced a page-numbering device; an assistant asked the simple question, 'Why cannot the paging machine be made to write letters and words, and not figures only?' And so the typewriter was born.

. . . but you only know if you feel them hit you on the head!

A variation on this technique can be used in association with the classical specification questions (what? when? where? extent?) either to clarify a problem or redefine it looking for novelty.

It also forces you to gather the information needed to answer these same questions. The technique asks:

What is at present achieved/proposed/required?   **And why is it . . .?**

Who?	**And why?**
When?	**And why?**
Where?	**And why?**
How many?	**And why?**

Working through these questions helps to break the problem down into component parts. You may achieve better understanding, better problem clarification, or problem redefinition.

(d) Use analogy and metaphor
Divergent people in particular often redefine problems by using

some form of analogy or metaphor. While such techniques are more usually found useful in group creativity situations, some individuals do find them useful when working alone. They provide a form of escape from the traditional approaches.

Let's look at an example. Suppose your problem was 'How to improve the efficiency of the sales force'. Perhaps it could be restated as 'How to make the sales force operate as effectively as the Wimbledon Football team in the 1988 F.A. Cup final?' This is an analogy, and could lead to thoughts about specialisation, about new training designs, about unusual team morale strategies, and about techniques for frustrating your competitors. Alternatively, it could be restated as 'How to make the sales force run more smoothly', leading to a metaphoric view of the sales force as a smoothly running engine. This might trigger ideas such as fuel supply (information aids), maintenance concepts (benefit programmes), turbocharging (e.g. incentive

schemes, or special meetings), and emission controls (e.g. compensation, order handling, etc.).

2. RANDOM STIMULI TECHNIQUES

This is anything that will jolt you out of your linear, conventional ways of thinking. They can be split into two kinds of stimulus. One kind is the physical – touch it, feel it, pick it up and look at it – the stimulus you might find when you go for a walk somewhere different. The other kind of stimulus is words – they can be powerful because of the meanings attached to them, and they are readily available! Both kinds are discussed here.

(a) Go for a walk somewhere different

Or visit a place you don't usually frequent. Find a trade exhibition, or visit a toy-shop on the way home. Try the local fair if it's on. And take your problem or opportunity or issue with you.

Even on your way to wherever it is you're going, let the signals, the events and stimuli that are all around you, into your head. The object is to expose yourself and your problem to anything which may act as a trigger for new thoughts and perspectives, new associations or new solutions. The new circumstances and surroundings provided by your walk, or your visit, are likely to provide unusual and unexpected triggers.

Why go somewhere new? Because a different environment, by its very 'newness', will have a greater impact on your thinking. You have also made a *conscious decision* to seek these novel surroundings as part of your search for solutions. Thus you are taking the important step of admitting that previous habits, previous information, previous ways of thinking, probably mostly left-brained, are not adequate, and that's why you need some new ideas.

The challenge of making new surroundings, with all the different things you see and hear, work for you is to see *how many* novel insights you can develop on your problem. The fact that the things you're looking at, or hearing, or touching, are some way removed from your problem is advantageous. They force you (if you let them) to examine the problem in new and different ways.

Persisting in seeking these new insights, and trying to link a particular something on your walk to your problem, requires you to move away from the old left-brained, ingrained habits of thought. The procedure encourages you to bring your right brain into play, and use *all* of your head's resources, both right and left!

Most of us have in our memory instances of when chance events or random 'thoughts' have helped us to solve a problem. A common situation is to be browsing in a newsagency, or a bookshop, or reading someone else's magazine while in a

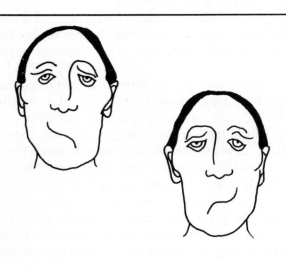

Which of these two faces is happier? In fact, they're mirror images. But most right-handed people usually select the top figure. This smiles on the left. What is seen in the right-field of vision is sent to the left-hemisphere, and vice-versa. Perhaps this is an example of judging with the right brain? Try moving the picture to your extreme left, and the extreme right. Any different response?

waiting room or on a plane, when suddenly – 'Hey, that's it!' A solution to a problem that's been in your head for days, weeks or months is suddenly there, triggered by something (apparently) quite unrelated in the magazine or book you've been looking through. Just what it was that produced this new answer doesn't really matter. Nor does the fact that there may be little 'logic' to it. What matters is that your new idea is

---

Try this now
Decide to give the next 8–9 minutes over to that problem that is worrying you and gets you home late. Select any object or device to use as a trigger, however much it may seem disassociated with the problem. Look around the office, look on the mantel-piece at home, look in a child's toy cupboard . . .

Ask yourself how this thing, and any ideas coming from it, can throw more light on the problem. Stay with it for 3 or 4 minutes. Don't let go – persist! Note down the thoughts that have come to you.

_____

_____

_____

_____

_____

_____

_____

Now find another, different, object or device, and use it in the same way. Force a link between the object, and your problem, and explore it. Even though it's not clear where it's taking you. Again, record your ideas.

_____

_____

_____

_____

_____

_____

_____

valuable to you. This sort of spontaneous triggering, or association, is really nothing more than your right brain getting into gear, and finding solutions independently of your more customary sequential thought processes.

Getting yourself into a situation where this can more easily happen, by 'going for a walk', is just one way of encouraging right-brain activity. You don't have to go out and walk, of course. The triggering process can be brought about by things that surround you right now. What's vital, however, is the way you use your head when looking around. If it's ideas you're after, then keep an open mind. Don't eliminate things because 'that could never possibly help'. Don't seek stimuli that seem to fit well into your problem's framework, or that look likely or comfortable (they won't get you out of your mental rut). Do be persistent!

(b) Random matching

Another way to force our way out of left-brain tradition and into more novel approaches is to substitute *words*, chosen randomly, for the events of the walk, or the toy-shop, or whatever. The thought process remains the same; the search for an association, or an insight, triggered by the stimuli (this time a word), may lead to new ideas or novel approaches.

You want a word? Open that dictionary, stab your pen at the newpaper, or turn ahead in this book and point at a word. Same request as before. Don't scan a page looking for a word that seems 'right', or easy. Make it random, and get your head to find the association, insight or answer for you. Force yourself. Looking for *associations* is important, and perhaps you will need to establish a series of them before an idea emerges.

The manager in the situation in the box on page 131 did not claim that the string of associations were restricted to the chain of words above. There were many more leads into other words but those leads were unproductive at the time. But he kept going, kept playing with words and ideas, unconcerned that he didn't quite know where it was going, until, quite unexpectedly, a potential solution was there.

RANDOM WORD = NEW PRODUCT RANGE

A manufacturer of domestic garden equipment wanted to extend its product range. One manager decided to try using random stimuli, and a dictionary as a source. He later described the process of association as something like –

Word from dictionary – 'glacier'
Associations were
'Glacier – ice – cold – hot – steam – smoke – fire – coals BARBECUE!'

The company subsequently agreed that barbecues and associated outdoor living products should be investigated as a possible extension to their product ange.

With hindsight, it's not hard to see how these 'irrational' trains of thought have led us to solutions for problems that are now behind us. Using hindsight like this can help us accept that the method can (and does!) work. And that's important, because when using associations on real problems, you don't know where they are taking you. So persistence is important, despite possible feelings of uncertainty. It's a process of exploration, and to make it work you just have to build some confidence and skill in the use of this simple procedure.

3. IDEA SEARCH CHECKLISTS

Why does it sometimes take many years for a simple solution to be found? The question is probably unanswerable.

What we do know, however, is that with some application of the idea-generating tools described here a person can stimulate him or herself into seeing new connections, new combinations and new answers. It is already clear from the earlier part of this chapter that questions are powerful aids. Alex Osborn developed a checklist which both helps expand our view of the problem and also leads to new solutions.[3] Osborn's key questions are:

Adapt? Modify? Magnify? Minify? Substitute? Rearrange? Reverse? Combine?

How simple solutions elude us . . .

Cards used for holding and machine-processing of data were first used in the USA, in the 1890s, for census work. The square corners of the cards became dog-eared with use, and caused some difficulties in handling and processing. With hindsight, the solution to the problem is simple. Round off the corners of the cards. But it took over fifty years for this simple solution to be thought of and implemented!

Other questions can be added to provoke further divergent thinking. For instance:

- What if it were upside down? – or inside out?
- What if the size were changed? – shape changed?
- What if the key feature were carried to extremes?
- Can it be smaller/bigger/safer/cheaper/faster/lighter/stronger?
- What could be left out?

Why not write out for yourself some challenging questions to ask yourself about a current problem? Or if you prefer, use the following questions developed from Osborn's work.

Adapt or borrow from elsewhere?

Where else can I look?	Like the studies of dolphins made by naval architects investigating the movement of ship hulls through water.
What can I find in history?	Like modern fashion designers bringing back old styles as new.
Are there parallels in nature?	Like the R & D group who designed roofs which changed colour (to absorb or reflect heat) based on studies of the chameleon.
What other ideas might be used?	Like the use of women's hairsetting lotions to put permanent creases into wool fabrics (wool being chemically similar to hair).

A GOOD IDEA – THE PORTABLE LABORATORY

An organisation with strong interests in applied research needed a portable laboratory for a protracted and mobile investigation. But money was tight. One of the technicians one day said 'How about a shipping container?' Knee-jerk judgment ('Don't be stupid!') was held at bay, and the idea explored. The group found out that containers used for shipping food were both refrigerated and insulated. And damage to the insulation, which sometimes occurred, made them unusable, and so available cheaply! Size was good – one would hold all the equipment without trouble. There seemed no reason windows and airconditioning couldn't be fitted – and portability was excellent for they were *designed* to fit onto semi-trailers/articulated lorries as well as railway cars. Perfect!

So it wasn't such a funny idea after all. One was in fact bought (cheaply!), modified and used successfully at a fraction of the cost of a purpose-built structure.

Modify or change in some way?

Change the shape?	Like king-size cigarettes, or queen-size beds. Or 'bricks' that are really just stick-on 'brick' tiles.
Change the presentation?	Like soft-covered books instead of hard.
Change the form?	Like detergent powders instead of bars of soap, or liquid detergents instead of either. Or water-beds.
Change the appearance?	Like fins on cars in the 1950s.
Add motion?	Like mobile underwater swimming pool vacuum cleaners.

Magnify?

More strength?	Like steel in concrete, and nylon in wool socks.
More capacity?	Like eight or nine-seater cars on a conventional saloon wheelbase.

Longer time?	Like slow domestic work-top cookers, which take all day to cook your evening meal.
More width?	Like the makers of certain car wheels and tyres.

'Minify'?

What if shorter?	Like Mary Quant and the mini-skirt.
What if frequency reduced?	Like the oil companies and longer service-interval car engine oils.
Collapsible?	Like umbrellas that fit into a briefcase or bag.
Smaller?	Like micro-sized domestic audio equipment. Or contact lenses.
Lighter?	Like reproductive fibreglass 'old beams' for house interiors.
Eliminate?	Like tubes from tyres, or 'heat' from microwave ovens.

Substitute?

Source of power?	Like solar for gas, or conventional electricity.
Another process?	Like stamping a metal part, instead of casting.
Materials?	Like truly liquid inks in new generation ballpoint pens.
Other ways?	Like plastic cards for money.
Other parts?	Like gas bottles for wood in domestic barbecues.

Rearrange?

Re-package?	Like so much on any supermarket shelf! Or like repackaging financial transactions, and leasing rather than buying, or using hire-purchase.
Change the sequence?	Like building the roof of a house first, and walls later.

Change the layout?   Like centre-turn lanes at many road intersections. Regroup? Like quality control circles.

A grandmother writes poems for young children. Popular ones are 'Sammy Snail', 'The Little Raindrop', 'The Swing', 'A Family of Rabbits' . . . and so on. She explains how she goes about creating her verse stories . . . 'I just imagine myself to be the little creature or thing I'm writing about. If it's a raindrop, then I'm falling through the sky like a raindrop. It it's a snail, then I become a snail. With that view of a sn*. "*s world, the words come quite easily.'

While this method could be labelled as a fantasy technique, it's really no more than someone using a method they know works for them as a way of being creative. The constraints of human left-brain 'logic' are easier to keep at arm's length when you're intent on becoming a snail!

The point is, it works, and it will work for managers, too. Got a problem with the filtration plant? Or the conveyor system? Or the viscosity of the mix? Imagine that you're in there – that you're part of the process, doing whatever it does. How does it look from the inside? How does it feel? What's happening to you when you're in there? And why?

New perspectives and insights created in this way can lead to solutions, or part solutions, or new approaches that would otherwise elude us. Try it for yourself – especially with technical or process-type problems.

Combine?

Mixing basic ingredients?   Like the various blends of natural and synthetic fibres.

Putting two required elements together?   Like a screw-on brush for the end of the hose, for car washing. Or selling ties and handkerchiefs in matching sets.

Bringing different skills together?   Like the investment advisory 'shops'.

Put to other uses?

This one is left for you.   How many ideas can you come up with for alternative uses of existing items, products or services?

Sometimes, the inspiration for a successful new product or service comes directly from observations in daily living. For example:

The idea

- *for cotton buds* came to Leo Gerstenzang when he noticed his wife wrapping cotton on toothpicks to clean their baby's ears.
- *for cellophane drinking straws* came to Otto Dietenbach when he was idly twisting the outer wrap from a cigarette packet around a thin steel rod.
- *for an outboard motor* was Ole Evinrude's answer to ice-cream melting in a boat he was rowing to a picnic on an island on a warm day.
- *for Diners Club* hit Rudolph Schneider one night when he was entertaining friends at a restaurant and found he had lost his wallet.
- *for the automatic toaster* was Charles Strite's answer to burnt toast in the lunchroom of the factory where he worked.

Of course, someone had to respond to the idea . . .

(Vesper, K. H., *New Venture Strategies*, Prentice Hall, 1970, p. 135)

This use of questions and imagination to encourage divergence can be further developed into a matrix format for use with a group. The simple matrix format allows differing responses from each group member to be recorded against each question, with the responses themselves becoming possible triggers for new ideas within the group. These alternative uses of checklists are described under the Idea Stretch and Idea Growth headings in Chapter 7.

4. SLEEP ON IT

This isn't so much a 'final' method for use by individuals as one which should be encouraged in parallel with the others. It's just what the heading says. Sleep on the problem. Periods on the edge of sleep, either 'drifting-off' or semi-awake in the mornings, can be very productive of ideas. These are periods when our language dependency is minimal, and when left-brain activity is either winding down or not yet wound up. Whichever it is, opportunities are there for some right-brain, divergent thoughts to surface. You can't consciously force it to happen, but you may be able to encourage it subconsciously.

The creative process within our heads is said by some psychologists to involve four stages:

1. Preparation
2. Incubation
3. Illumination (insight, or 'solution')
4. Verification (checking it out; evaluation)

While this is too passive a view for us to find useful, it does make the point that sleeping on it or 'incubating' the problem and your preparatory work on it is part of the overall process. Our work with managers and Mindmix demonstrates that in practice this incubation period can be very brief. Insights can come in minutes, and sometimes even seconds. But it's useful to remember that when all else fails – and even at other times – 'sleeping on it' can still be productive.

Idea Banks – for keeping track of ideas

How many seemingly good ideas did you have last month? And how many of them can you reproduce now? If you're like most people, you will have lost some along the way. They've just been forgotten.

To avoid losing them, establish some kind of record-keeping system. Ideas are unpredictable. They come upon you at all sorts of unexpected times. Unless you have a simple system, and make recording them a habit, you will continue to lose more than you'd like.

Carrying a notepad or a few index cards in your pocket or purse is not hard. Recording the essence of an idea without trying to evaluate it usually takes very little time. For current or future projects, set up idea banks, one per project. The bank may be only a file in a convenient drawer, or a box or a miniature tape-recorder. What it is doesn't matter very much as long as it's easily accessible. Ideas can then just be 'banked' as they come to you. The few moments required make the eventual problem-solving task so much easier. When you do need to take action on that particular issue, your idea bank will contain the accumulated thoughts of the previous weeks or months.

One Inventor we know who won an International Inventor of the Year Award, keeps a note pad beside his bed. On waking up through the night with an idea, he can quickly record it for elaboration or evaluation the next day, or 'idea-bank' it for consideration later.

As we've said, many people report ideas occurring when on the fringe of sleep, while waking up, and sometimes while under the shower. These are all situations where language dependence is minimal, and it seems possible that with the language-centred left brain off duty while asleep, or close to sleep, the right brain and its more divergent thoughts becomes dominant. The experience described in the box above will be shared by many others. Idea banks simply help systematise the recording of those divergent thoughts. A pad and pencil on the bedside table or a portable dictation machine in the car are often all that you need to get your banking procedure started.

The two important 'rules' mentioned at the beginning of this chapter remain, whether you are working alone at developing your divergent ability or working within a group. They are the rules of suspending judgment, and delaying evaluation.

New ideas, like plants in the garden, take time to grow to maturity. If you demand too much of your young idea, through premature judgment and evaluation, it will very possibly be killed off. Worse, you will be denying yourself the chance to develop fully your own creative skills, as premature judgment and evaluation both suppress your divergent potential.

For now, when you are in the idea-generation phase, give your imagination free rein. Judgment of your ideas, and evaluation, and other left-brain centred censoring activities, come later.

On the sometimes advantage of not knowing too much about why that idea can't work . . .

'All of my biochemistry colleagues whom I told said it wouldn't work. I had the advantage of knowing nothing about protein chemistry – and it does work!'

A senior CSIRO scientist commenting on his new way of synthesising certain chemicals for use in drug manufacture.

(CSIRO, *CoResearch, Australia*, April 1984, No. 270)

Moral: **You don't care how you got the new idea – just so long as you've got it.**

7

Creative Tools for Groups

> Many Involved Xpressly

Individuals moving into a group, whether it be an 'ideas group', or some other kind, bring with them their own perceptual 'apparatus'. They all view the world in their own special and different way. Given an open-ended problem, group members will respond with different ideas or solutions. If you'd like to try this, take a sheet of paper drawn up into squares (as on page 142). Ask each member of a group to name the squares, to write into each square a title for what it could be, to think of squarish things and write their names down, one per square. Give them only 3–4 minutes. Then have each read out his or her list in turn, with each subsequent group member eliminating what has previously been read out but revealing the total number of squares they have named. Typically, you'll get a range of named squares from 8–28 in 4 minutes, and total for a group of ten of about 100 different names. Some will be very conventional (e.g. a TV set, a window) but others will be very divergent (e.g. a person, a cross-section of a timber beam, etc.). The range will surprise you (it always surprises us), but this simple exercise will prove the point: groups can give many more ideas than any one individual.

'Defrost before Cooking'

To move groups into creative modes typically requires some preparation of individuals. They come together somewhat defensively – and who wants to be the first to make a fool of himself/herself in front of the others? They come together somewhat formally, from within the bureaucratic structure of their organisation, highly conscious of each other's title, position and supposed power – a clear series of warnings to stay left-brained, to be careful and conservative! They come together because of someone else's problem (for instance, yours), and might be otherwise quite busy – and clearly their right-brain processes stay with the problems they've left behind!

For all these reasons, it is desirable to precede any attempt at innovation via groups with some relaxing or opening-up activities. These are typically called 'defreezing' activities. (Hopefully, they remove *all* the frost!)

Defreezing activities can be as simple as the blank squares exercise mentioned earlier, or as complex as a structured exercise forcing people to meet, to talk, to joke. It doesn't really matter; even the DPA device used with a new group with open and friendly discussion of the meaning of results has been used successfully. We've even managed it with a short description and discussion of the left-right brain model, but we're careful to keep it light and *humorous*. Why humorous? Well, we know that social and emotional activities are essentially right-brained, and we are trying to move people into at least a divergent mode of thinking. Small groups that laugh a lot, that have fun, do seem to have an advantage in the fluency of idea flow.

Defreezing also provides an opportunity for discrete reassurance of true divergent thinkers in the group. 'You see – we laugh *with* each other, not *at* each other's ideas!' 'You see – you're allowed to be different. There's no right or wrong answers.' While these may not be expressed explicitly, they'll certainly be implicit in the ground rules established during any effective defreezing stage.

Not all inventions/innovations are accidental or come from chance questions or odd associations. But where they're not, the basic idea often already exists.

- **Dynamite.** Basic idea: safe, easily manageable replacement for nitroglycerine. Alfred Nobel is reputed to have spent over ten years tracking it down.
- **Oxytetracycline.** Basic idea: an antibiotic with a broader spectrum than penicillin. Pfizer Inc. (USA) sponsored a world-wide collection of soil samples to test for spores, a methodical and determined effort.
- **Diesel engine.** Basic idea: an engine which would be more thermodynamically efficient than a steam engine. Rudolph Diesel spend fourteen years developing his engine design.
- **Vaccination.** Basic idea: an old wives' tale; 'I'll never have smallpox because I've had cowpox.' Edward Jenner tested this concept for twenty years before actually vaccinating a person.

Groups which are used to both creative processes and to meeting with each other clearly need less intense defreezing. However, we would still take a few minutes to relax everyone, even with an experienced group. They need a chance to move from the convergent pressures of their possibly routine existences to the divergent demands of the innovative group.

A special note here: one form of defreezing is in effect pre-training. In this, groups are fully prepared for their divergent roles. This is, of course, the most successful – but the most complex – method.

Playing Chef

Flexing the collective creative muscle – that is, working with groups for new ideas and other innovative intents – imposes some unique responsibilities on you, the manager. If too many cooks can spoil the broth, there's no doubt that an inattentive chef might be left with nothing in the pot.

One of the major responsibilities is protecting the flow of divergent ideas. In any of the methods/tools which follow, care must be taken to create a safe environment for divergent thinkers, or not-so-divergent thinkers who are self-conscious about this trip into the right brain. This is not a difficult responsibility; it mainly means avoiding judgemental situations and delaying evaluation. Much of the message of Chapter 3 is important here.

Other responsibilities include:

- Ensuring adequate defreezing.
- Selection of appropriate tools to assist the group (and the rest of this chapter should help here).

A QUICK CHECK – HOW CREATIVE IS *YOUR* TEAM OF PEOPLE AT WORK?

Idea rich groups	*Idea poor groups*
1 FLUENCY – *number* of ideas offered	or, does your group offer few ideas?
2 FLEXIBILITY – *variety* of ideas offered	or, is your group rigid, offering ideas today much like yesterday's?
3 ORIGINALITY – the novelty, or uncommon-ness of the ideas	or is your group 'me-too-ers' offering up the same tired old stuff?
4 AWARENESS – curiosity, or 'insight' . . . their concern for exploring the new	or is your staff blinkered, suffering 'job blindness', and not seeing opportunities because they've stopped looking?
5 DRIVE – or just being determined to make that new idea really happen	or do you suffer from low commitment?

If your groups are nearer the descriptions on the right than on the left, then you certainly need to keep reading.

- Knowing when to stop. Idea-generation groups, in particular, can have off-days, and may burn out quite quickly. Persevering when there's no sign of divergent activity is a waste of time. Abort, and try again later, is the safest rule.
- Providing a common process for keeping a group 'on the track'. It isn't true that to be innovative we have to be irrational. (Nor is it true that rational processes must be bureaucratic.) However, it is common that open brainstorming or other intuition-dependent devices are used when a new idea is needed, and similarly common that the 'formal' rational processes (e.g. lateral decision-making) are saved for big decisions. Both approaches are wrong. Many rational processes lend themselves as innovative aids. For example, evaluation of futures should trigger opportunities – if it doesn't then there's not much use worrying about innovations; you won't be there to need them! The rule of thumb is: Use what works. And if it helps by keeping people on the track without killing divergence, it's good!

Idea-generating Tools

In the rest of this chapter we will look at various tried and proven processes to generate ideas and/or recognise innovative opportunities. All of Chapter 6 is relevant to groups (as groups are made up of individuals) despite its individuals' heading. The emphasis in this chapter is on idea-generation (but not exclusively; some of these techniques can also be used for opportunity recognition). The processes are arranged in a sequence of simple-but-useful through to more complex processes. The more complex are not necessarily more useful.

The processes described are:

- Slip/card writing
- Brainstorming (and variations)

- Semantic processes (idea stretch and idea growth matrices)
- 'How to' sessions
- Structured systems:

  (a) Attribute listing
  (b) Decision process systems
  (c) Matrices
       (i)   Two-dimensional matrices
       (ii) Multi-dimensional matrices

- Excursion techniques
- Combination tools

SLIP/CARD WRITING

Why do most groups appear uninventive? The answer is clear: no one has ever handed them an 'idea tool kit' and shown them how to use the tools to better their lives and work.

Most of the carpenter's tools we use are simple. A screwdriver is a single shaft with a handle and a dull blade. Nor is there anything very complex about a saw, hammer or chisel.

Slip writing has the same simplicity. It can be used to collect a large number of ideas from any meeting in just a few minutes. Even the shyest person expresses ideas without fear of ridicule, because the method preserves anonymity. No one knows who offered each idea. It thus sidesteps the competition that sometimes happens when some members of a group try to outshine others. And it produces a pile of ideas in a form that allows fast sorting into categories for action planning.

The method is simply this. Everyone at a meeting receives a pad of, say, twenty-five 8 by 14 cm slips of paper or cards. The leader presents a problem statement in 'how to' form. For example, 'How can the local Chamber of Commerce improve its services to members?' The leader then explains the importance of holding back judgments and asks that each person write down as many answers to the question as the time period will allow. Each answer must be written on a separate slip or card, and the time given for the task, after the explanation has been made, need only be 4 or 5 minutes.

The leader should prepare for the slip-writing session by walking the whole process through in his mind several times. Explanations should be rehearsed and then edited for brevity and clarity.

Although any facet of a problem or opportunity works for slip writing. 'How can we ---' questions yield the highest returns on a first effort. Specificity is golden. 'How can we help field personnel provide better reports on competitive activity?' will give a better payoff than, 'How can we improve our competitive knowledge?'

If a specific question is impossible, don't hesitate to use something more general. A first 'general question' round of slip writing can produce the specific subquestions for later sessions.

Plan the logistics. Provide each person with a pad of slips. Have extra pencils ready and prepare a method for collecting the slips. Boxes or cartons placed at strategic points can serve as idea banks.

The explanation should be no longer than five minutes. Tell the group that they are going to participate in a new type of problem-solving that will produce 60 to 100 (or more) new ideas. Then introduce the question and explain its importance. The participants should try to get a flow of ideas going. Each idea should be written on a separate slip. Stress there is no need to evaluate the ideas or to write supporting rationales. Thoughts such as 'We tried that already' or 'This may be illegal' should be put aside. Encourage the group to write quickly, and remind them that they have only 4 minutes to generate the ideas and write them down. Pausing or hesitating suggests some censoring (left-brain) activity. Before and *during* the slip writing, keep hurrying people and telling them to write the first thing that pops into the brain, then the next, then the next, etc. 'Don't stop to think; you're already thinking. Write whatever comes into your head.'

HUNTING GROUNDS FOR IDEAS

PEOPLE
PEOPLE
OTHER PEOPLE
MORE PEOPLE
AND THEN, TRY MORE PEOPLE

Slip writing works! Time after time we've seen new ideas emerge. The basic rules are:

- Keep the 'how to ---' problem as specific as possible.
- Protect anonymity.
- Keep the pace up.

Some exponents of this technique suggest 10-minute sessions. We get very good responses in 4 minutes.

Successful examples are many. Possibly one of the simplest was a retailer caught with excessive inventory of garden tractor mowers. The problem was 'how to sell increased numbers of mowers without loss'. An inexperienced manager, who had never before used slip writing but had seen one demonstration, was sent into one of the company's stores to form a quick group for slip-writing. He selected four girls in the lingerie department (they were the first group he encountered), explained the problem and had them write slips for four minutes. Even without defreezing, and despite the probably narrow experience range of the group, he received a bundle of ideas. At least four of these were considered totally new *and* implementable. Not only was the retailer able to move the excess stock, they established a new level of continuing sales.

Of course, slip writing need not be limited to 'how to' questions. Any stage of management activity can use the method to advantage. For example, it can be used in a prospective manner, to find opportunities and future potential problems. A group can be asked to write slips about 'clouds on the horizon', say 6 to 12 months ahead. The anonymity of slip writing protects people who wish to raise insecurities, and these insecurities may be important future concerns.

Suspending judgment and delaying evaluation has been previously raised as critical for encouraging divergent thinking. Almost all applications of slip-writing observe these principles, but a '**murder board**' breaks it. A murder board is a specific use of slip writing to find out what might be wrong, or what could go wrong. For example, after a series of ideas has been evaluated, each risk individuals see can be recorded on a slip. This is a quick way to collect many risks or threats to the ideas' viability.

Many other variations of slip or card writing are possible. For example, slips can be passed from person to person, each writing two for one received thus encouraging an exponential growth in idea flow. Or they can be used as trigger devices for brainstorming. This simple process is limited by your imagination only. Why not ask a group for other ways to use this simple tool? (But ask them to put their ideas on slips.)

BRAINSTORMING (AND VARIATIONS)

Brainstorming is a generic term to describe any sort of meeting in which individuals are deliberately encouraged to offer ideas on a particular situation, usually an open-ended problem. In other words, everyone is free to say what they think and it will be heard and recorded. Brainstorming sessions do seem to work to some degree, probably because:

- The power of association is like a powerful two-way current. One idea from an individual almost automatically causes him or her to think of another idea or spurs the imagination of a second individual. A feature of creative output appears to be seeing new relationships, piecing together otherwise unrelated phenomena. The opportunity for this to occur is obvious in brainstorming.
- The stimulating effect of people voicing ideas in groups (almost in competition) increases idea-generation. But this is probably only in the left brain and is more for the 'point scorers' than the divergent thinkers.
- Brainstorming provides reinforcement and recognition by rewarding all ideas with receptiveness.
- An environment is created which provides all participants with 'psychological safety' --- it's okay to be divergent.
- Studies show 'free associations' of ideas are (over 90 per cent) more numerous in group activity than when the individual works alone.

There are five basic rules for brainstorming:

- Rule out criticism. Evaluation has no part in a brainstorming session.
- 'Free-wheeling' is welcomed. Even wild ideas are heard and recorded.

- Quantity is encouraged without reference to quality. The more ideas, the greater the likelihood of useful ideas.
- Listen to others' ideas: look for combinations and linking of ideas and improvements. Piggyback your ideas on others.
- All ideas offered are recorded without censoring (and this is best done where the record is visible to all participants).

For groups experienced in unstructured techniques (e.g. an on-going 'value analysis' group), pure brainstorming sessions may be useful. But consider the sessions you've been on in the past:

- Have they been totally non-censoring?
- Did other 'secondary goals' seem to emerge for some individuals? (e.g. 'I'm sure I can give the most ridiculous suggestion', or 'I'm bound to impress the boss; I haven't stopped giving ideas since this started.').
- Did the really 'odd' thinker, the true divergent, start to open up?

Or was the brainstorming a game in which the same people who give the ideas on a regular basis continued to be the idea-givers? There is no right or wrong way to run a brainstorming session as long as the five rules previously listed are followed. But the reasons that sessions so often fail and just produce a large number of low-quality ideas seem to be:

- The environment conducive to contributing (that is, non-threatening) is not established.
- The leader becomes an informal censor; 'I'll just summarise that ---', or 'that's similar to ---' are censoring statements.
- Many times the leader has an idea he or she is in favour of, and the brainstorming session becomes more of a manipulation session.
- The lack of structure permits 'secondary goals' to become important.

- There is no deliberate attempt to draw out the 'odd' thought from potentially divergent individuals. Even where we recognise them, in the spirit of the brainstorming game we ignore them.
- The purpose and relevance are not made clear to participants.
- The problem being worked on is too 'general' for brainstorming to be effective, or not sufficiently open-ended.
- Or the problem is too narrowly defined, so the group doesn't get far enough away from the conventional.

Good brainstorming sessions start off with a defreezing activity, a deliberate appeal to the motives of the group and the relevance of the subject, a clear statement of the situation to which ideas are directed, and an open statement of the rules of the 'game', particularly no censoring.

If you are trying brainstorming, expect ideas to flow slowly at first, but build up momentum by recording as quickly as possible and constantly requesting – 'What's next?', 'Who's got another?', 'Can we build on that?', etc.

So you want to brainstorm? Then try the following:

1 Set the climate; use an exercise to build trust, legitimise the 'odd' idea, build confidence. *up to 1½ hours*

2 Check out that you are really working on the *right* problem. *5–15 minutes*

3 Have a practice session, on an irrelevant, light 'practice' problem. *3–5 minutes*

4 Brainstorm your issue. *10–15 minutes*

5 Extend ideas using a 'wild' one as a trigger, or by putting some ideas on to slips and swapping them around the group. *5–10 minutes*

6 Ask individuals to develop further ideas from what is already recorded. *5 minutes*

It is a useful idea to run a brainstorming session with the same group on the same topic twice, but separate in time. The first session will help the truly divergent individual to see there's no ridicule involved.

There are many variations to brainstorming. The more common are:

- **The Gordon technique.** In this technique the leader starts the discussion with some of the concepts basic to or closely associated with the problem or decision. He then stimulates the discussion, and reveals the true situation when the group is close to a satisfactory solution.
- **Cascade sessions.** Each group member is given one of the ideas so far generated, and asked to write new ideas silently, triggered by the one given, on top of a notepad sheet. After three minutes each person hands their pad to their neighbour, who then uses these top-of-the-page ideas as triggers, or stepping stones, to some more new ones. After another three to five minutes (how busily are they writing?) pads are handed on one last time.
- **Trigger sessions.** Start with slip writing. At the end of four minutes each group member reads out his list, triggering others present into more new ideas on more slips. Sometimes the triggering can be encouraged to develop into verbal, group brainstorming to alternate with periods of individual slip writing. Note, however, that this method removes the anonymity of slip writing, and so needs to be introduced differently.
- **Catalogue technique.** A commercial catalogue, trade directory or telephone book (yellow pages) is used as a source for ideas. These, in turn, may suggest further ideas, or trigger new approaches.

SEMANTIC PROCESSES
Some of these were covered in Chapter 6. The techniques of redefinition and random matching, and the use of the Idea

Stretch Checklist are as relevant for groups as for individuals.

There are two other proven lists of questions, similar to and somewhat overlapping with, the idea stretch checklist which we have found useful with groups. These are the Idea Stretch Matrix and the Idea Growth Matrix (see tables on pages 155 and 156). We use either of these to follow up on 'that's-a-good-idea' comments in a particular field, the assumption often being that if that reaction is expressed there's possibly some opportunity lurking. We call these 'matrices' as opposed to 'checklists' since we use them in groups, and record individuals' reactions in the available spaces. Anybody can contribute to any gap in the matrix; not all gaps are filled, for not all questions can always be answered. Using idea growth and idea stretch matrices in pairs before involving the entire group is a useful process. The pairs seem to force each other to provide answers and, with an appropriately pre-trained and/or defrozen group, they prevent each other from discarding the 'way-out' answers.

IDEA STRETCH MATRIX

Insert *idea of interest* here ⬆			
Who else can use it?			
What else can I do with it?			
Where else can I use it?			
When else can I use it?			
How else can I use it?			

IDEA GROWTH MATRIX

Insert *idea of interest* here			
What if . . . It were made bigger?			
What if . . . It were made smaller?			
What if . . . It were reversed?			
What if . . . It were combined with . . .? . . .?			
What's a possible substitute?			

Both idea growth and idea stretch matrices are deceptively simple. But these proven question series have produced some novel ideas. Here are two from recent groups:

- Self-drawing curtains. A special self-recoiling spring unit at the end of the curtain rod, which withdraws the curtains when they are pulled slightly. This was a response to 'where else can I use it' for a group investigating retractable electric power leads.
- Toy slot cars – that don't fall off. A slot car electric track designed with a partially closed U shape, with the slot cars with an inverted 'T' shape peg. This was a response to 'What if it were reversed?' for a group investigating track lighting fittings.

'HOW TO' SESSIONS

These are a special class of the semantic processes, and are well suited to semi-technical problems or opportunities. 'How to' sessions are useful where something has been going wrong, and the cause is known but simple corrective action is for one reason or another not available. New alternative actions, usually adaptive in nature, must be found.

'How to' sessions are best conducted in small group (8–10) people. They need an objective leader, a 'client' (the person with the problem), and the other participants as the 'creative resource'. The following is a summary of the process:

1. The client is asked: 'Tell us your problem in one sentence beginning with the words, How to'. This sentence is recorded on a chart or board.
2. The participants are asked: 'Write down on a piece of paper all the different ways you see this problem, also beginning with the words, How to'.

    'How to's' may be partial, inaccurate or distorted. They may even incorporate approaches to solving the problem. None are rejected.

3. While the participants are writing, ask the client questions to provide some input to the writing groups. Questions such as those that follow are typically used:

    'Give us some background to the problem.' 'How did it get like this?' 'Why is it your problem: what's your part in it?' 'What have you already tried or thought of trying, and why haven't you been successful?' 'What would you like from an ideal solution?'

4. The participants are then asked to give their statements of how they see the problem, or how they would solve it, beginning with the words 'How to'. Record as many of these as possible on a flip chart or board. If an interesting or unusual approach is offered, ask for more detail. The client may, of course, contribute 'How to's' if any occur to him or her.

    In recording 'How to's', do not censor. Get as many different 'How to's' as possible.

5. The client is then asked to select a specific statement, one that seems most promising or most interesting, and to explain why he/she has picked that particular one.

6. The participants are now moved towards solution thinking: 'Any ideas or the beginning of ideas which might move us toward solving the client's problem?'

7. The client is asked from time to time to summarise what he or she has heard. This is a simple check on understanding.

8. From Step 6: 'What do you like about the idea?' This is an attempt to stretch the client a little beyond easy and obvious responses.

9. The client should also be asked, 'What don't you like about the idea? What's wrong with it; what do you want that the idea doesn't offer?'

10. The leader keeps recycling back to the participants looking for other ideas which build on the original idea but which will overcome any stated difficulties.

11. Steps 7–10 are cycled through until a possible solution to the problem begins to emerge, or until it is clear that the line of thought will not work. (If the line of thought is

unproductive, the client can select another 'How to', or you can try another technique.)

12. When the client feels enthusiastic or satisfied with an idea, it is useful to record answers to the following questions (using a flip chart or board):

'Describe the possible solution to your problem. Why do you think it will work for you, and what can you do with it?' Use the group to check that nothing important has been left out.

'How is this solution new for you?'

'What are the next steps (including dates, actions, persons, etc.) you will take to implement the idea?' Although the question is directed at the client, participants sometimes contribute here.

Sometimes it is a useful step to ask the group for possible solutions before starting Step 6. If there are some well-developed ideas at hand, it is useful to get them out quickly. It might not be necessary to go through the idea building process.

The pitfalls in using 'How to's' when criteria are loose are:

- Trying to solve too general a problem. It can't be done. Be specific.
- Not recording the proper information or recording information when it is not necessary.
- Getting bogged down in rambling shop talk.
- Stopping with one possible solution. The point of the process is to come up with as many solutions as possible.

STRUCTURED SYSTEMS

Not only intuition-dependent systems are useful for generating new ideas. Often, structure can assist a group. The major alternatives are attribute listing (or functional analysis) and decision process systems.

Attribute listing

This is a helpful method when needing ideas for extending, modifying or improving a product or a service. It requires that:

- A list of each component of the (say) product is produced, in factual, physical terms.
- A list of each attribute of each component is produced.

This is a very structured approach, but without it we are likely to see our product or service only in terms of what it is used for at present, not what it is capable of doing. That is, the structuring can aid subsequent divergent thinking.

The function of each attribute is then described and listed; that is, the answer to the question, what is its purpose?

A suitable example is a saucepan (1 litre size – aluminium). Working through this procedure gives us the following table:

Component	Attribute	Function
Container or body	10 cm high, 18 cm diameter, cylindrical, flat bottom, simple lid closure, cast aluminium, rigid, coloured	to contain a given quantity of liquid/ liquid + solids, stable when standing, full or empty, prevents vapours escaping, robust, conducts heat well, permanency, aesthetic appeal
Handle	projects from one side, hand-sized, plastic	ease of holding when hot, easy movement, easy grasp and movement, durable, heat-resistant
Lid	centre knob, heat-resistant, held in place by gravity, slightly convex shape	ease of lifting with one hand, simple to remove contents, prevents escape of steam/vapours

It's easy to see that many questions can be asked of both attributes and function.

Is the metal used appropriate to the required robustness and durability? Are lids necessary on all saucepans? Is one handle the best solution? Are heat-conducting properties just as required? Might light weight and low cost compensate for less durability and aesthetic appeal? A look around a saucepan display in a store shows that many of these questions have been answered by saucepans of new shapes, various 'casserole' dishes, double-handled saucepans, transparent 'glass' saucepans, and so on, each offering some change in one or other of the traditional attributes.

An alternative name used sometimes for this approach, functional analysis, reflects the possibility of focusing more strongly on function than on attribute, when this is appropriate. Yet another alternative focuses on the cost of meeting each functional requirement, and this method is known as value analysis.

Decision processes

Rational decision-making, where one idea is to be chosen from many, depends on having available a list of criteria against which the various alternatives will be assessed. Once a problem has been clarified and defined and the relevant criteria against which alternative solutions will be judged have been decided, then placing both the defined problem and the criteria before a divergent group can stimulate a flow of ideas. In order to avoid bias in the group, prompts from the leader as to possible solutions or existing alternatives should be avoided. Groups will commonly use brainstorming to develop ideas for testing against the criteria, and slip-writing and 'how-to' sessions may also be used. The structure of the criteria list probably acts as a constraint for convergent thinkers, but oddly enough seems to act in quite the opposite way with suitably defrozen divergent groups. We strongly suggest that you keep criteria setting as a separate activity.

Matrices

The distance charts on airline and road maps are the simplest form of matrix. The information is presented in the form of a chart, with cities listed across the top and repeated down one side. The boxes of the chart show the distance between any two places.

As a creative tool, matrices use 'ideas' or 'elements' in place of cities. And, unlike distance charts, the ideas and elements that run across the top are usually different from those down the side.

Matrix charting does not result in sudden creative insights, and will never replace individual divergence. But matrices can stimulate minds to see new relationships. A matrix chart can make associations happen. The search for associations is removed from the sole control of the right brain and made visible. This visibility assists group interactions required to generate new and novel associations or ideas.

Two-Dimensional Matrices. Perhaps the simplest matrices are charts on which variables can be juxtaposed. Often, problems or opportunities present with two obvious variables. Expressing these on a matrix gives an opportunity for looking for 'not-yet-done'. Of course you must be careful not to pre-judge possibilities; some of the associations may look odd.

An example of a two-dimensional matrix is shown on the opposite page. It's a matrix looking at the marketing of potato crisps, and the two variable dimensions being juxtaposed are packaging and flavour additives. As you can see, a list of packaging alternatives has been produced on one axis, and a list of flavour additives on the other. (Neither are suggested as complete, nor are they believed to be highly original.) These two lists, in practice, would be produced by two groups – not necessarily experts in the field of either packaging or food technology. 'Experts' sometimes find it very hard to break into divergence in their own field.

Groups could produce lists of possibilities to include on these axes by brainstorming, by slip writing or by any of the other processes that encourage divergent thinking. If you are a manager hearing some apparently strange suggestions, remember don't judge them too prematurely – some of them might just be very worthwhile. These axes are best completed by your

TWO-DIMENSIONAL MATRIX: Marketing of potato crisps

Packaging	Flavour additives										
	Salt	Salt/vinegar	Onion	Bacon	Garlic	Steak	Herbs	Chilli	Sugar	Brandy	etc.
Opaque plastic bag	▨	▨		▨							
Clear plastic bag							?				
Cardboard box	▨	▨	▨								
Opaque paper bag	▨										
Opaque plastic box											
Clear plastic box											
Plastic tub											
Foil bag	▨	▨		▨							
Cellophane tube					?						
Plastic bowls											
Film-covered trays						?					
etc.											

people. Allowing them a say in the formation of the matrix is an important step toward encouraging a sense of ownership.

Once the lists have been prepared, the 'already done' areas are marked out. This is shown by hatching in our example. Then the group is free to use the 'not yet done', of which there are 110 in our example, for possible ideas. They approach this in the divergent mode. Perhaps individuals make 'gut-feel' choices, or perhaps groups choose. However achieved, these choices are described with a brief explanation of why they appealed. No judgment or evaluation is yet attempted. Ideas are rounded out only by the question 'How could we do this?' In our example, it is suggested that 'herbal-flavoured crisps in a clear plastic bag', 'garlic-flavoured crisps in a cellophane tube', and 'steak-flavoured crisps in a film-wrapped tray' are ideas worth pursuing. Perhaps answers to the 'How can we do this?' question, often collected via slip writing, could suggest:

- Coloured herbs to make an attractive display of crisps in a clear plastic bag.
- Garlic crisps in small sizes as 'nibbles' at a premium price in a small cellophane tube, easily held in one hand.

Want to raise some money? Try a matrix.

Matrices can be used for 'services' just as readily as for 'products'. We recently ran a brief session on idea-generation at an educational institution. Educational funding is tight these days, and the topic chosen by the group was 'How to raise additional funds'.

This was soon improved to 'How to raise additional "resources"', as receiving an additional person for a year, or a piece of equipment, is equally as valuable as extra funds.

The matrix created by the group in twenty to thirty minutes contained over 500,000 ideas! Even accepting that as many as three quarters of these could be already known, or impractical, a rich potential remained.

And ideas about 'raising resources' are supposed to be difficult to find! Well, it depends how hard you want to try!

- Steak-flavoured potato sections, quite large and steaklike in appearance, presented in a film-wrapped tray as a meat substitute.

Why not create a two-dimensional matrix for an opportunity or a problem in which you have an interest, and see how many 'not yet dones' you can find?

Multi-choice matrices. Many problem or opportunity areas contain many variable dimensions. It is not overly difficult to build a variables matrix to help generate novel solutions. Two examples are shown here (pp. 166 and 168).

Linking up through the matrix can be done procedurally, or individuals' intuitive preferences can be accepted for further (and later) evaluation. An example of linking is shown in the second example.

Variables matrices typically produce enormous quantities of potential ideas. They also produce a great deal of rubbish. Obviously, having access to several million recorded alternative ideas in only a few minutes creates problems for screening and evaluation. Our experience suggests that in a typical multi-choice matrix:

- 20–60 per cent are previously known combinations. They are either in use, or have been thought of.
- 20–40 per cent are rubbish. (For example: from the example on page 168 'honey as a gravy in a paper bag for the home-hostess market'.)
- 20–40 per cent are totally new.

Often a starting point is best found in what is now done. In the example on page 166, the entering sentence describes an attempted programme to market excess jumbo-jet seats by an international carrier. The entering sentence provides the variables, and they can be temporarily eliminated to provide a 'broken sentence'. The potential elements to fill each hole are then listed. This listing can be done by either a convergent or

Entering sentence:

To fly family groups from Sydney to Bali at children-free fare for holidays.

Broken sentence:

To fly (market segment)	from (origin)	to (destination)	at (fare level)	for (purpose)
family groups	Sydney	Bali	children-free	holidays
retired couples	London	Singapore	'super-Apex'	shopping
singles (under 25)	Hong Kong	Hong Kong	10 per cent discount	sightseeing
young marrieds	San Francisco	Sydney	premium for	restaurant tour
cricket enthusiasts	New York	San Francisco	special services	sporting event 'special'
equestrians	etc.	New York	etc.	multiple tour
gourmets		London		etc.
schoolteachers		Samoa		
etc.		Tokyo		
		etc.		

EXAMPLE:
To fly **singles** from **New York** to **London** at '**super-Apex**' fares for **special nightlife tour**.

divergent group. Your choice really depends on the nature of the variable being handled. Clearly, if it's something very finite, such as 'all cities where a Boeing 747 can land', then a convergent group might be preferable. But if it's something less definite, and there should be more than one of such in any problem tackled by variable matrix, then a divergent group to make the listing should be preferable.

In a typical situation, *many* ideas can be produced by multi-choice matrices – often 2 million. And 20–40 per cent of 2 million is still a substantial number of new ideas. But care should be taken not to eliminate apparent rubbish too early; some of them may well respond to 'how can we make this work?' So, potentially, multi-choice matrices can reveal as much as 80 per cent of the total volume of ideas as new. In practice, we rely upon intuitive, divergent judgments to select potentials from the matrix. This tends to be a visual process, as illustrated in the example on page 168. More formalised evaluation is not possible, nor desirable, at this stage. Besides, we're only looking to find ideas, not *all* ideas, and we're not as yet interested in judgment or evaluation.

The difficult step in multi-choice matrices is getting a good sentence to identify the variables. Starting without a sentence is difficult; variables simply listed are not always interrelated in the way they are in a simple sentence structure.

In our management development activities, we challenge groups that they can produce 2 million ideas in 4 minutes on business problems they've never seen before – and the 2 million ideas will be recorded. The response is usually disbelief. But we then pose the problem, reveal the variables, and use the structured variables approach and have subgroups assist by preparing lists of options for each variable. We use a problem with six variables, each of which is capable of producing between 10 and 20 options. Since the total number of ideas equals number of options (variable 1) × number of options (variable 2) × number of options (variable 3) and so on, our challenge is fairly safe. We've never failed yet.

Purpose: To locate a new food product to capitalise on a newly developed cooking process

Processed (FOOD PRODUCT) as a			(PRESENTATION) in a	(PACKAGE) for a	(MARKET SEGMENT)
Meat	**Fish**	**Dairy**	preserve soup	dip bottle	infant
beef	mullet	yogurt	muffin sherbet	bread wall dispenser	children
lamb	crab	cream	consommé cracker	biscuit jar	teenager
mutton	lobster	butter	jam cake	icing shrink-wrap	over 65
sausage-meat	cod	cream cheese	dressing burger	sausage box	all ages
mincemeat	squid	…	topping bun	stuffing tube	campers
pork	caviar	…	spread waffle	drink 'boil-in' bag	fishermen
chicken	oysters	…	gravy pancake	pudding cup	non-smoker
turkey	whiting		wafer pastry	steak paper wrap	aviator
…	sardines		patty chip	loaf …	…
Vegetables	**Fruit:**	**Miscellaneous:**	candy custard	pie…. …	…
mushroom	watermelon	honey	… …	… …	…
tomato	banana	spaghetti	… …	… …	…
beans	passionfruit	macaroni	… …	… …	…
peas	fig	cashew nuts	… …	… …	…
zucchini	orange	curry (mix)	… …	… …	…
asparagus	avocado	margarine	… …	… …	…
potato	apple	…	*etc.* *etc.*	*etc.* *etc.*	*etc.*
…	…	…			
etc.	*etc.*	*etc.*			

EXAMPLE:

Processed **banana** as a **spread** in a **tube** for the **children's** market

   (food product)   (presentation)   (packaging)   (market segment)

(Note: Nature of process is irrelevant to the example.)

Not all multi-choice matrices reveal millions of ideas. Maybe you'll only get thousands. And not all are finished in four minutes; maybe yours will take a week of part-time work. But several thousand new ideas in a week isn't all that bad!

A nutritional company completed a multi-choice matrix to seek additional uses for a particular base product they possessed. The analysis revealed almost 1 million possibilities, several hundreds of which were considered viable.

Finding 'good ideas' can be easy – with the right tools.

Other structured matrices. Several forms of 'new product matrices' using pre-determined axes are in use throughout industry. A section in the Further Reading at the back of the book is devoted to this. We personally do not feel they are either idea-generation devices or total innovation tools, but rather situational analysis tools, so we do not go into detail here.

EXCURSION TECHNIQUES

When the more normal processes of idea building do not give satisfactory results, one or another form of excursion from the problem may help. An excursion is useful when you are really stuck.

An excursion is a trip away from the problem into a line of thought that has little to do with the problem. The idea is to stimulate divergent thinking, which is hard to do when you are concentrating on the point where you are stuck. By departing from the core of the issue and generating a climate of detachment, of 'playing around', it may be possible accidentally to discover a new thought.

Here in summary is one form of excursion:

1. State the problem as a 'How to . . .' statement on one flipchart. Leave this up to one side throughout the excursion exercise.

2. Select a key word from the statement of the problem. The key word should be one which is as suggestive, interesting and concrete as possible, and which can lead thought away from the problem (as it is stated). Write the key word on a second flipchart.

3. Ask the participants to tell you anything the word suggests. Ask one at a time, with each person building on the previous comment. Write down the list of associations on the second flipchart as it develops.

4. Select a word from the list. Remove the list and write the new word on the flipchart. Again select the word which gives the participants the best chance of leading themselves away from the problem.

5. Ask participants to construct a fantasy on the word, and write the fantasies privately on a sheet of paper.

6. Try to build a group fantasy starting with one person's and adding to it, one at a time, or have several fantasies described without connecting them.

7. Write down the key elements of the fantasy or fantasies from step 5 as participants describe them. (If the group is having trouble getting away from reality and into fantasy, interrupt at critical moments with outrageous questions. Build towards fantasy.)

8. Repeat steps 5–7 until everybody is away from reality.

9. When it is apparent that the entire group is in fantasy (everybody's having fun and the words/elements recorded have no obvious connection with the original problem), quite suddenly ask the group to move back toward the real problem and offer a connection between any of the last recorded elements and the real problem. You're trying to jolt a right-brain connection. Accept even a seemingly absurd connection. These are typically called out, but they may trigger a thought in another group member.

Excursion techniques are not difficult to use, and they're certainly not as ridiculous as they might sound if you've never experienced them.

AN EXAMPLE OF AN EXCURSION

A group was attempting to solve a problem of material sticking to the walls of a rotating mixer in a chemical plant. Previously several convergent approaches had been tried, with limited success.

The group leader decided to use an excursion as a way of taking the group away from their problem. It had been with them for several weeks and the leader felt they were just 'too close to it' – too locked into ideas already known to them. The leader took a key word from the problem definition – 'lumps'. He then asked the group to offer any thoughts about lumps from the world of nature, choosing 'nature' because of its distance from the chemical plant. Ideas generated included:

Mountains
Rocks on the bottom of a stream
Animal droppings
Cancerous growths

Again to create a distance between the problem and the group, the leader asked what it felt like to be a rock on the bottom of the stream. Some responses were:

Always cool
A very pleasant place to be
Rarely disturbed
Impossible to breed

The leader then followed on the 'permanent' issue (seeing its possible relation to the problem) and asked the group 'What would be necessary to move you, when you're a rock on the bottom of the stream?' Replies included:

Cross-country hikers
Dynamite
A flash flood
An earthquake

The leader next asked the group to associate these ideas with the original problem: the 'flash flood' seemed immediately relevant. Could the sticking material be washed off? The technical manager, who was present, confirmed that additional water in this problem situation was no barrier, because of later centrifuging.

The solution for testing was reduced to the simple idea of installing a high-pressure water hose to remove the sticking material as necessary, as the mixer rotated. That is, flash-flood it.

Subsequent testing confirmed that this was quite practical, and obviously inexpensive.

They sometimes work — and in the area of generating novelty, sometimes is better than never. We tend to save them for when we're stone-walled, and the problem is relatively closed, although presented in an open-ended manner. Excursions don't give a great range of ideas; once a good connection has been recognised, groups typically concentrate on this one. But again, one is better than none.

Excursions are often very helpful on technical problems such as the one described in the box on page 171. They force a distancing from well-known technical aspects, and raise the level of speculation. New product development is another area where excursions can be valuable, although they can also be used with problems in administration, marketing, cost-reduction, personnel, etc.

> An aluminium manufacturer had produced a large inventory of foil trays. The market demand for this size of tray had virtually disappeared. What to do with the inventory?
>
> A simple slip-writing exercise produced several hundred possibilities. The process took approximately four minutes. Ideas ranged from 'oil trays for garages' to 'shipping containers for crayfish'.
>
> Using slip writing to solve small marketing problems is easy . . . and quick.

Combination of idea-gathering tools

Please don't view the idea-generation tools as discrete processes. They typically tie together. For example, slip writing can be used for triggers to brainstorming. 'How to' sessions can follow from opportunity recognition achieved by one of the simpler semantic systems. There's no correct combination; the basic rule of thumb is still valid — what works, works!

The literature on creativity is full of names for processes and systems to aid idea-generation by groups. Morphological analysis, for example, is a complex title for systems such as multi-choice matrices. Other titles are proprietary; for example, Synectics is a title for a process in part combining 'How to—' sessions and other processes (e.g. excursion techniques).

Be wary of complex labelling of idea-generation tools and creativity devices. It is easy to complicate these simple devices by labelling and by insisting on 'correct' approaches. They're all simple ways to:

- Help divergence emerge.
- Try to get access to the right brain.
- Increase quantity of ideas or find an idea where none is readily apparent.
- Suspend judgment and delay evaluation.
- Capitalise on varying cerebral styles in groups, and the synergy this provides (that is, use the whole brain or 'Mindmix').

The best way of illustrating that these methods can work for you is to try them. A summary follows. Keep trying, and you'll be surprised at how many novel ideas you and your group can produce. It's almost always fun, and most of the time it's productive.

A finance company was keen to increase it's market share of loans. Following extensive training of middle management in idea-generation, idea-evaluation, and idea protection/ improvement, idea groups were formed. Two significant ideas emerged from among many. One was a concept of promoting in foreign languages, specific to large migrant groups. The other was a method of redefining loan applicants' disposable income, both to simplify applications and to make eligibility fairer. The consequence was that the company achieved a substantial increase in market share . . . it moved to first place!

Trusting the idea-generative capabilities of its employees paid off for this organisation.

IDEA-GENERATION CHECKLIST

Common label	Comment	Space for your comment as to relevance or usefulness to you
1 Slip/card systems (a) Slip writing	Very useful process. Requires no elaborate tools or strong leadership skills. Can be used on very large groups.	
(b) Trigger sessions	Almost any device can provide a 'trigger' for entering into brainstorming and informal opportunity or idea discussion. Slips can be particularly useful here.	
(c) Round robins	A simple variation of slip writing where slips are passed from person to person to 'kick off' additional thoughts.	
2 Brainstorming sessions (a) Osborne ('classical')	Limited to smaller groups. Some difficulties with group dynamics and controlling mild ridicule. A proven technique, but usually unable to produce vast numbers of ideas. Very good for permitting new associations to be seen.	
(b) Cascade sessions, trigger sessions	Sessions with this name are usually of the brainstorming variety, and use other devices (e.g. slip-writing pads) to provide triggers for discussion, or for new ideas individually generated.	
(c) Catalogue techniques	A name sometimes used to describe brainstorming sessions using pictorial matter (e.g. catalogues) as triggers.	

3	Semantic processes	
	(a) Redefinitional techniques	Covered in Chapter 6 as a group of individual tools, any or all of which can be used with groups. The technique can be summarised as:
		(i) 'Ask around it' (ii) Challenge the boundaries (iii) Worry it with 'Why?' (iv) Analogy and metaphor
	(b) Random matching	Random word-to-word, to trigger new associations. Covered in Chapter 6, but can be used with groups.
	(c) 'Idea search'/'Idea growth'/ 'Idea stretch'	Checklists of questions to encourage new thoughts. Often successful with small groups (2–4 people).
4	'How to' sessions	A controlled group servicing a 'client', the one with the problem or need. Good for finding a 'different approach', but often a little stilted in application and not leading to a wide range of new ideas.
5	Structured systems	
	(a) Attribute listing (or functional analysis)	Attributes of a thing taken singly, and potentials listed. Can be similar to 'morphological analysis' (see below). Often includes some brainstorming.
	(b) Decision processes	Essentially, using a structured criteria list as a frame of reference for a possible divergent viewpoint.

continued overleaf

IDEA-GENERATION CHECKLIST – cont.

Common label	Comment	Space for your comment as to relevance or usefulness to you
(c) Matrices (morphological analysis)	(i) Charts Two-dimensional format. Excellent device for opportunity recognition where two variables can be identified. (ii) Multi-choice matrices Handling many variables. There's often a difficulty in creating the 'broken sentence'. Generates many alternatives, and creates problems for screening.	
6 Excursion techniques	Using words and/or situations to lead away from 'the problem', and from reality. There's usually a 'jolt back' when a new idea or new association is seen. Often, closes down on one idea.	
7 Combination tools	In idea-generation, people use what works. There are many brandname combinations (e.g. Synectics), but anything may be used and may be useful if it leads people to: (i) get access to their divergent thoughts (ii) communicate their divergent thoughts (iii) see new associations (iv) 'trigger' from other people's thoughts (v) accept the unusual from others (vi) break out of the traditional/conventional thought processes.	

8

Handling Ideas Once You've Got Them

Maximising Integrative Xchanges

Managerial effort must necessarily be aimed at action. Having powerful idea-generation tools, building groups to unleash divergent thinking and access the right brain, and generally stimulating innovative thinking via organisational strategies, is all very well. But it's of no use unless some of the outputs lead to action. And that can't happen unless ideas are screened in some way, unless more useful ideas are separated from less useful, and unless decisions to implement are made.

As noted earlier, multi-choice matrices can yield millions of potential ideas. Screening and evaluating millions of alternatives is no easy task. Now, the main thrust of this book is stimulating innovation, so we're not going into fine detail on the screening, selection, idea protection/improvement and planning processes. They need an entire volume in themselves. But it would be impossible for us to ignore these processes completely. Our message would be incomplete. We've seen innovative programmes falter because the follow-through from excellent idea-generation, and the generation of excellent ideas, just didn't happen.

Accessing the right brain, and generally stimulating divergent thinking, may be new to many managers. But it's not difficult and it's also not sufficient for innovation. Yes, it's necessary if you are to find truly novel answers. But you need to evaluate, improve and protect new ideas to be ready to implement them. And that means you're involved with whole brain processes – that is, with both hemispheres and with people of both convergent and divergent strengths. You're involved with Mindmix.

The broad dimensions of the innovative process can be viewed as:

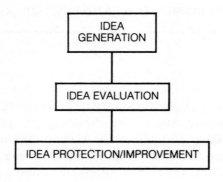

What triggers this process? Sometimes just innovative intent (e.g. 'Let's get our strategies right!'). At other times, it clearly is recognition of an issue or concern facing a group or organisation. This could be a problem issue (e.g. 'Something's gone wrong!'), or a decision situation (e.g. 'What will we do about . . .?'), or a strategic concern (e.g. 'Which direction to go . . .?'), or an operational concern (e.g. 'What promotional theme . . .?'). In some instances, the focus might simply be triggered by one person coming up with an isolated 'good idea'. Of course, the only reason we recognise it as a 'good idea' is it fits our stated or unstated understanding of an issue/situation/concern/opportunity. This relationship is demonstrated in the stylised flow of the innovative processes (page 180).

Screening for Potential Winners

If you use the techniques suggested and described in the two previous chapters you'll have little trouble in getting new ideas. Alternatives that are novel, and at face value exciting or worrying, will become the least of your concerns. Sorting the chaff from the wheat, the potential winners from the 'also-rans' and 'impossibles', will be much more of a pressing issue. The relationship of idea-generation to the other elements of the Mindmix process is shown in the diagram of the overall flow of the process. Idea evaluation is shown to consist of two stages, a screening stage and an actual evaluatory (selection) stage.

There are almost certainly two levels of screening in any evaluatory or decison-making model. One is very much a part of the decision-making or selection step. This formal sense of screening is criteria-based. But the other comes earlier. It's a primary screening device to produce a shortlist, or a refined list of potential ideas. This is usually intuitive. Sometimes, it employs screening lists. It's called **preliminary screening** on the flow diagram. Preliminary screening can be with or without lists.

The human mind treats a new idea the way the body treats a strange protein; it reject it.

P. B. Medawar, biologist
quoted in Byrne, R., *The 637 Best Things anybody ever said*,
Sphere Books, 1984

Screening without lists

Where a particular problem or opportunity has been identified and adequately clarified and defined, and specific project groups have been assigned to work on the problem or opportunity, it is not unusual to receive a very large number of ideas in a short time. In such situations, criteria screening lists are

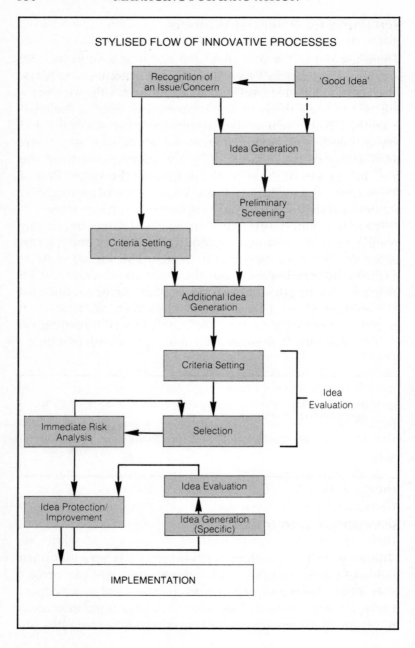

STYLISED FLOW OF INNOVATIVE PROCESSES

insufficient or too time-consuming for preliminary screening; there are simply too many ideas. Where you have a great number of ideas to screen, processes which further capitalise on the intuitive judgment of people in the organisation may be preferable. Managers spend a great deal of time performing lip-service to participation. Management theorists praise participatory methods, but rarely describe a simple one. Well, here's the simplest: *Ask your employees.* It's so simple, and it's so powerful. And it's basic to the total Mindmix approach.

If you've got several hundred ideas for a particular project, what could possibly be wrong with shortlisting down to the 5–10 most popular with your employees by seeking their opinions, and then further evaluating these? To some, this will clearly suggest the possibility of the loss of the 'best' idea. But you can't lose what you haven't found. And further, a 60 per cent good answer with 100 per cent commitment is every bit as good as a 100 per cent good answer with 60 per cent commitment.

Gathering employees' views can be done through groups, by a questionnaire device, or by some sort of competition. It doesn't really matter. What matters is the involvement and feelings of commitment you're likely to generate. Of course, not all employees may choose to participate, but many will. The strength of this process is clear when you hear (as we have) people say – '*We* helped design/choose/develop (whatever) that product', or '*We* decided/planned (whatever) to do it that way'.

A special warning here. Don't just ask your managers; they're probably mostly left-brained survivors of the educational obstacles. Unless they've been through appropriate development experiences, they've probably not learnt to trust their own right-brained, intuitive judgments, let alone the 'hunches' of others. (Even reading and understanding this book and the principles and pragmatic approach of Mindmix may not be sufficient.) Go down. Ask the people who might really be able to contribute some intuitive judgments. Ask salespeople; ask office personnel; ask storemen.

Dick Smith, first man around the world solo in a small helicopter, primarily made fame and fortune in retail electronics. He used this method to select which new products should be stocked from the wide range available. His screening device was his sales staff. Sales staff were given a list of possibilities, and a great deal of information about them, and asked to vote on whether or not the stores should sell the products. Dick Smith ran with the ones they nominated.

(*Financial Review*, 2 August 1984, p. 1)

In summary, a way to preliminarily screen large numbers of ideas is to ask relevant people what they like, and what they think would be 'good' or appropriate. It is a simple message. Of course, give them sufficient description of the problem or opportunity, and perhaps your major criteria, to make them comfortable and to help them make a more relevant choice.

Screening with Lists

Different organisations have evolved different devices to affect preliminary screening. On pages 183 and 184 are two examples of screening lists. The second shows a weighting system. They both provide an estimate of whether the idea should be hurried along, forgotten, or perhaps more data is needed. Devices of this type are not decision models; they set screens to eliminate ideas which might otherwise look 'good' but are irrelevant given the things important to the organisation. They are a sort of 'loose' convergent approach.

In practice, we find such lists best employed where isolated ideas are flowing occasionally. They provide a 'quick-and-nasty' indication of whether it is worth investing additional management or development time and effort. A relevant situation would thus be where idea teams (by whatever name) have been in place for some time, have overcome the initial

SCREENING IDEAS (1)

The following is an example; it is the way *one* organisation goes about screening. It handles isolated ideas (essentially of a product nature), and yields a 'probability of success' concept.

Factor	Score
Invented inside company/organisation	
Offers performance advantage	
Offers price advantage	
Uses special, existing, manufacturing skills	
Uses markets in which we're already active	
Raw materials requirements as now used	
Use processes currently used	
Protected technology	
Extended existing range	
Has brand or trade name strengths	
Uses specialised plant/equipment (existing)	
Uses present distribution channels	
Uses specialised distribution methods (existing)	

Note: Screening methods such as this do not differentiate well between competing ideas. Simple scales (such as this one), because of the binary nature of scoring, are limited in practical application

Score 1 point where the idea fits a factor. Interpret total score as:
0–4 chance of success less than 15 per cent;
5–8 chance of success less than 60 per cent;
9–13 chance of success as high as 80 per cent

euphoria which may flow from divergent opportunity, and have a diminished but realistic idea flow. Another would be where a 'suggestion scheme' approach to finding ideas is in place.

Selecting a Winner

Evaluation is never totally convergent; we all make intuitive judgments daily without being able to support our choices or opinions easily. Divergent activities, such as the employee-

SCREENING IDEAS (2)

The following is an example; it is the way *one* organisation goes about screening. It handles isolated ideas, and yields a 'proceed-further' concept.

	Weight	Score	Score x Weight
Compatible with company image and overall business policy	10		
Profitability	9		
Fit with marketing competencies	8		
Market permanence	8		
Size of market (potential scales)	7		
Fit with existing manufacturing capabilities	6		
Incremental capital investment	6		
Exclusivity and protection	4		
PERFECT FIT:	580		

NOTES:
1 Such screens raise questions, e.g. What is 'ideal' for profitability?
2 A common variation is to have two sets of criteria: positive (contributing to value) and negative (weaknesses).

60 per cent or better proceed to detailed study;
40–60 per cent call for further information and other similar alternatives;
less than 40 per cent, reject

based preliminary screening techniques, have a respectable role within management of innovation. But screening can be a relatively convergent task, as exemplified by the formal lists seen earlier. Evaluation also implies screening, but more formally. This permits only the valid to be considered for selection.

The difference between decision-making approaches which stress rationality and the evaluation step within the Mindmix approach is:

- The so-called rational decision models stress convergence; they reinforce established left-brain competencies.
- The Mindmix idea-evaluation gives full value to the

divergent processes, but without detracting from necessary convergence; it uses the whole brain.

The Mindmix approach is contrasted in a diagram (on page 186) with the more convergent decision approach. Referring to this, you can see that the heavy emphasis on idea-generation throughout the process provides a balance between those activities which are dominantly convergent and those which are dominantly divergent; the whole brain is active through the whole process.

At the risk of seeming repetitive (but it's important enough to run the risk), most traditional management methods are convergent. They place 'analysis' on a pedestal and worship it daily. They pay homage to 'analytical skills'. Their practitioners are left-brain experts. They probably even laugh at the concept of 'intuition'. But, of course, they'd be laughing at Einstein, Leonardo da Vinci and many of the other great break-through thinkers of recorded history! In the rational decision model it is usually emphasised that criteria be established as soon as the decision purpose is clarified. The argument normally mounted is that, if criteria are set after ideas/alternatives have been found, the human tendency to manipulate will surface, and the criteria will favour some particular alternative. This is a sort of back-handed acknowledgement of right-brained intuition; yes, somebody for some reason which is not clear is attracted to alternative X, but we better make sure that this 'gut feel' is not allowed to grow!

In the Mindmix approach such intuition-based alternatives are encouraged. In fact, we strongly suggest you keep criteria setting as a separate activity. We delay it until a good range of

---

The only reason some people get lost in thought is because it is unfamiliar territory.

Paul Fix quoted in Byrne, R.,
The 637 Best Things anybody every said, Sphere Books, 1984.

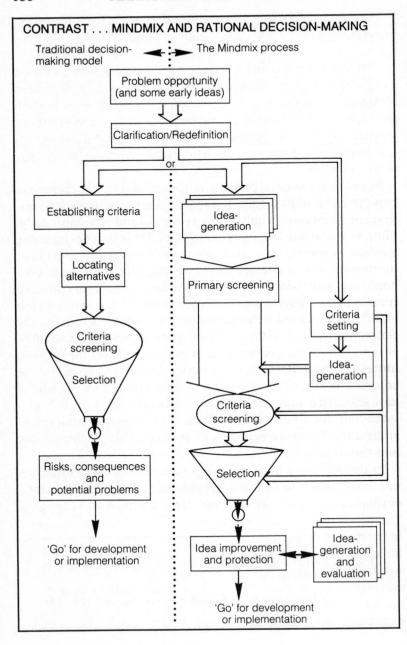

CONTRAST . . . MINDMIX AND RATIONAL DECISION-MAKING

Quite difficult matters can be explained even to a slow-witted man, if only he has not already adopted a wrong opinion about them; but the simplest things cannot be made clear even to a very intelligent man if he is firmly persuaded that he already knows, and knows indubitably, the truth of the matter under consideration.'

Leo Tolstoy, *The Kingdom of God is within you*, 1893

intuitive responses have been elicited. Why? Well, from our experience of encouraging managers and supervisors to opt for innovative alternatives and to apply decision-making techniques, we see fewer fresh ideas where criteria are set and exposed early. Now, our joint experiences cover many thousands of individuals and hundreds of assignments, so we don't feel our observations are merely superficial. It's as if the criteria list constrains many people, keeping them in the left brain. We've seen the same phenomenon many times in idea-generation. Somebody raises some quantitative data and, however brief the discussion of this data, the flow of ideas diminishes sharply. The criteria put an immediate constraint on people's minds, and their capacity to develop divergent thoughts is reduced.

The message is fairly clear. At any point in the innovative process where your intent is to look for new ideas, don't confuse those looking with facts! Facts, to them, are likely to be seen as constraints. We've stressed this under different labels in this book — we've called it suspending judgment, delaying evaluation, putting idea-generation ahead of idea-evaluation. The labels don't matter. What does matter is, if you've been lucky enough to get a group operating into right-brain thinking for new ideas, don't jolt them back to the left brain until you need to. It's hard enough to get some people out of their convergent mode once, let alone twice, in the life of one management issue. The rational decision models and the idea-evaluation step of Mindmix have much in common. Two deci-

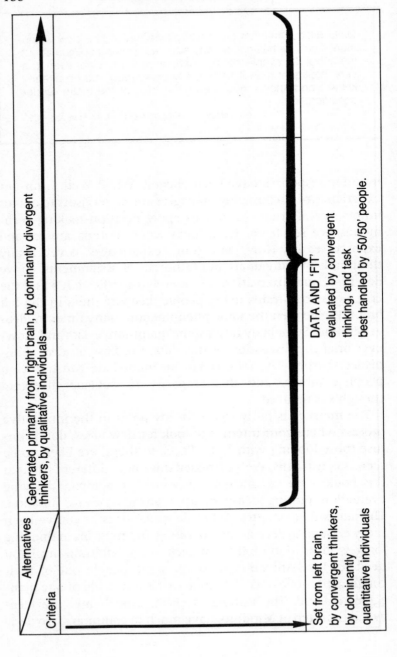

Alternatives

Generated primarily from right brain, by dominantly divergent thinkers, by qualitative individuals

Criteria

Set from left brain, by convergent thinkers, by dominantly quantitative individuals

DATA AND 'FIT' evaluated by convergent thinking, and task best handled by '50/50' people.

IDEA-EVALUATION (1)

Below is an example of a decision matrix used to evaluate four new-product concepts. Please note: not all factors have been included.

	Weight* (W)	ALTERNATIVE IDEAS											
		A			**B**			**c**		**D**			
			Score (S)†	S × W		Score (S)	S × W				Score (S)	S×W	
Absolute criteria:													
Within investment capabilities		✓			✓			✓		✓			
Within business strategy/policy area		✓			✓			✗ outside our business area		✓			
Comparative criteria:													
Maximum profitability	10	(data)	10	100	(data)	3	30			(data)	7	70	
Maximum sales potential	9	(data)	6	54	(data)	10	90			(data)	8	72	
Maximum 'fit' with existing plant	6	(data)	8	48	(data)	10	60			(data)	4	32	
Minimum disruption to existing business	5	(data)	9	45	(data)	4	20			(data)	10	50	
				247			200					224	

*The figure in the weighting column is an indication of the relative importance of that criteria. We suggest you assign a weighting of 10 to the most important criterion and adjust the weighting figures given to other criteria in proportion. There is no absolute right or wrong about this. It is another managerial judgment, but one probably best taken by the person who has the final responsibility. Weightings tend to reflect policy directions and are usually not amenable to participative decison making. The person whose neck is on the block and who stands or falls according to the outcome of the decision is the one who should state what the priorities are.

†The figure in the score column is a measure of how well the particular data fits the relevant criteria. Often a 10–0 scale is used, with 10 representing the best fit and others scoring relative to the 10.

IDEA-EVALUATION (2)

Below is an analysis used to evaluate four new-product concepts. Please note: not all factors have been included.

NEW-PRODUCT ALTERNATIVE/IDEAS

	Weight (W)	A		B		C		D	
		Score (S)	S × W	Score (S)	S × W	Score (S)	S × W	Score (S)	S × W
Positive factors:									
Potential sales	10	6	60	4	40	5	50	2	20
Using surplus manufacturing capacity	6	8	48	2	12	7	42	1	6
Exclusivity	4	2	8	5	20	9	36	8	32
TOTAL POSITIVE			116		72		128		58
Negative factors:									
Human resource difficulties/conflicts	6	4	24	1	6	6	36	6	36
Marketing complexities	4	2	8	2	8	4	16	1	4
TOTAL NEGATIVE			32		14		52		40
TOTAL POS. MINUS TOTAL NEG.			84		58		76		18

sion matrices are shown as examples (on pages 189 and 190). They are only slightly variant; the lateral model is essentially the standard format for the evaluation of alternatives. Within the Mindmix approach we stress this same lateral layout for the evaluation step for three major reasons:

- It permits process visibility; individuals can not only see their individual contribution, but they can see where the evaluation has got to, what step has been reached.
- It permits simple combination of the secondary (criteria) screening step with the selection steps.
- It provides a simple matrix for discussing the relative contribution of:

  > left brain *vs* right brain
  > convergence *vs* divergence
  > 'quantitativeness' *vs* 'qualitativeness'

This is important in pretraining, but also to keep the different strengths in a typical group 'up-front'. It helps remind individuals what mode of thought is desirable at this point. This matrix is summarised in the table on page 188. (This is not a text on decision-making. It is not our intention to detail step by step the processes and difficulties of idea evaluation. This is available elsewhere – please see Further Reading).

Growing new ideas and keeping the birds off the fruit

Once a few ideas survive the evaluation process, they are still not safe. To repeat an earlier analogy: think of new ideas as small seeds whose progression to mature plants will require careful nurturing. Young ideas, like seeds, are sensitive. They can be easily damaged and too easily overlooked. Sometimes they are poorly formed as well as sensitive. They will need pruning, spraying and fertilising if they are to produce their best. And they are often born into an environment where predators are everywhere – all too ready to destroy.

Too often, it seems like open season on new ideas. And the predator or hunter population is very large in most organisations. In fact, there are usually more idea-hunters than idea-conservationists. And idea-hunters seem to want to kill *anything* that's different. Its potential is of no concern to them.

There is a need to ensure that the young idea's early life is protected, that the hunters are either kept at bay or converted to conservationists. The process for doing this, the idea improvement/protection element, is a definitive whole-brain process. It needs both convergent and divergent thinking almost concurrently.

Idea improvement and protection are aimed at securing the future. To keep a new idea alive means looking towards its future, seeing what might happen to it. And if there's anything a manager is paid for that separates him/her from others, it's looking ahead. Surveying the future for opportunities, threats, potential disruptions, added resources and new activities should take up a good proportion of your time. When a new idea is involved, it's imperative that adequate future surveying is undertaken.

On page 193 is a diagram on surveying futures. It shows clearly that a 'futures survey' may have an origin in threat, or an origin of a more positive nature. As the diagram shows, these are not very different phenomena. Every threat recognised is a potential opportunity. Every analysis to improve a plan, to minimise the significance of potential problems, must by its very nature be a form of opportunity analysis.

We all know that if anything can go wrong, it will. And we all know that if nothing has gone wrong, something is about to. And new ideas *are* very sensitive; they're usually among the first things affected by Murphy's Law. (Murphy is alive and well. He has now established a global network!)

Planning ahead and building defensive and contingent plans are simply not enough. What is needed is penetrating and divergent activity at each step to make sure adaptations and

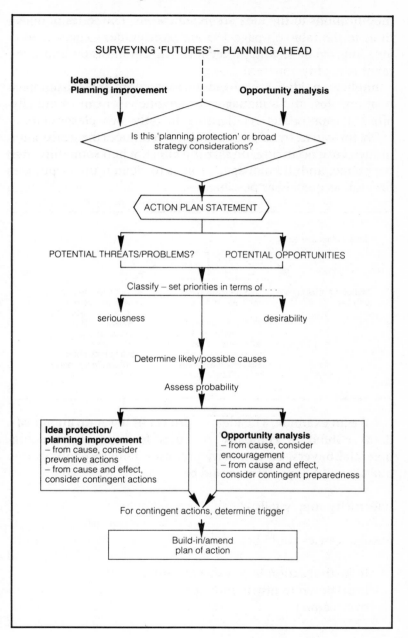

SURVEYING 'FUTURES' – PLANNING AHEAD

**Idea protection
Planning improvement**   **Opportunity analysis**

Is this 'planning protection' or broad strategy considerations?

ACTION PLAN STATEMENT

POTENTIAL THREATS/PROBLEMS?   POTENTIAL OPPORTUNITIES

Classify – set priorities in terms of . . .

seriousness   desirability

Determine likely/possible causes

Assess probability

**Idea protection/
planning improvement**
– from cause, consider
preventive actions
– from cause and effect,
consider contingent actions

Opportunity analysis
– from cause, consider
encouragement
– from cause and effect,
consider contingent preparedness

For contingent actions, determine trigger

Build-in/amend
plan of action

modifications to the idea are *improvements*. The series of questions in the table on page 195 are basic guides to getting into idea improvement and protection. The emphasis on improvement is readily apparent.

Implicit in idea improvement/protection are cause-effect relationships, and a manager (or anyone else) can essentially affect a cause/effect relationship in only two places: either *before* the cause, by taking action which reduces the probability of the cause occurring, or *after* the effect, when something *has* happened, and the manager's role is to clean it up, or put the fire out, as quickly as possible.

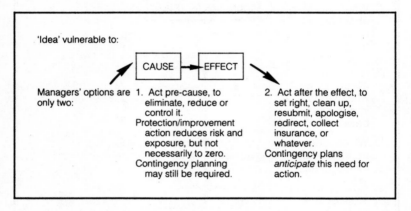

Take an example: The idea, or project, is to set up an out-of-doors exhibit of company products for trade buyers and potential buyers, on company premises. One response to the question at A (opposite) would be:

'Electricity supply fails —'

Possible causes could be:

- industrial action in power authority
- breakdown in distribution grid
- overloading
- ???

	Thinking involved	Support process
A What might happen/go wrong?	Either left or right brain. Divergent thinking an advantage.	'What if . . .' questioning, similar to the system described in Chapter 7.
B What are the effects, and what are the possible causes of each of these?	Both left and right brain. Convergent and divergent inputs equally sought.	Data and opinion collections. Slip writing and/or brainstorming are useful here.
C What can we do about these causes, if anything? Can we prevent them, or reduce the probability? How can what we do improve our basic idea?	Right brain. Divergent thinking is needed.	Slip writing. Brainstorming. 'How to . . .' matrices.
D Which ideas from C are best for our needs.	Left brain. Convergent thinking desired.	Screening and idea-evaluation.
E How do we capitalise on this problem or effect if we can't do something about the cause?	Right brain. Divergent thinking is needed.	Slip writing. Brainstorming. 'How to . . .' matrices.
F Which ideas from E are best for our needs?	Left brain. Convergent thinking required.	Slip-writing. Brainstorming. 'How to . . .' matrices.
Total	Whole brain.	Virtually all idea-generation and idea-evaluation process.

Prevention measures possible are:

– for industrial action? None. Outside our control. The risk remains, so contingency action needs to be planned to cope with the possible effect. A part of the solution might be to have a standby generator available on site, ready to run. Which contingency improves our exhibit? How?

– for breakdown in distribution grid? Similar.

– for overloading? Here a manager could act to prevent the cause occurring, as it is 'internal'. Checking demands for power, scheduling peak loads or restricting power available to some sections would be possible ways out. A manager may be satisfied that such actions eliminate risk to the project from this cause. Planning has contributed to protecting the project. If the manager's judgment is that some risk still remains (some 'effect' may still be felt), then contingency planning is required. Perhaps iced coffee, tea, or champagne from ice-boxes, to compensate for the hot coffee no longer available? Or portable gas burners to maintain a supply of hot refreshments? Here's the start of *improvement* thinking. And a lot of it is divergent.

The use of idea-screening, idea-evaluation, and idea-improvement/protection is a critical link is using the whole-brain resource of a group. In these processes the convergent thinkers and their quantitative skills are brought back into perspective. Divergent thinking is not more important than convergent thinking, it's just different. Certainly, it's vital for idea-generation. But idea-generation for idea-generation's sake seems somewhat futile. For Mindmix, there must be both sides of the brain active; both divergence and convergence at work. Each has a role.

Part 3

MINDMIX

Application

9

How To Get Started In Your Organisation

> ### Mindmix In Xecution

What do you do to start a deliberate innovation programme within your organisation? What should you be careful of? This Mix attempts to answer these questions, and provides sound practical advice for moving forward. We have set it out so that you may use it in a practical way to make notes about your own organisation.

On page 200 is a diagram of an installation process for a total innovation programme. This is generalised, but it's not theoretical. It's a practical, tried and proven model. Of course, being a generalised and somewhat simplified model, it's had a pruning; we've had to, without mercy, cut some of the branches and small tips from the main tree. For example, there are many feedback loops which we would normally consider important, but space, simplicity and desirable generalisation all favour this briefer version.

Clearly, every organisation is unique. Your organisation may well have features, personalities or activities which will force adaptation of the generalised installation model. The idea is, of course, to make the model fit your organisation, and not the other way around! What follows is a listing of the steps to work through in getting a Mindmix approach to innovation started. In outline they are

Step 1 Commit your top management group.
Step 2 Recognise or define your initial opportunity or problem areas.
Step 3 Identify relevant people.
Step 4 Train the people from Step 3.
Step 5 Multiply the effort.
Step 6 Keep track of it.
Step 7 Reinforce it.
Step 8 Extend the process.

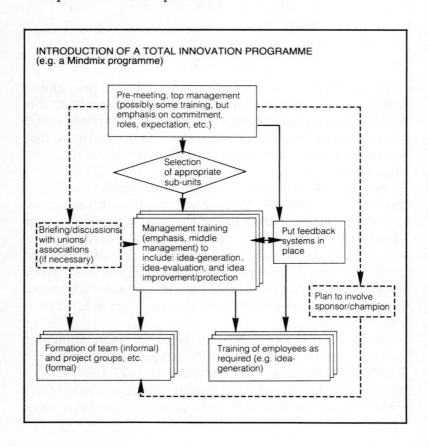

INTRODUCTION OF A TOTAL INNOVATION PROGRAMME
(e.g. a Mindmix programme)

BANK YOUR IDEAS HERE

Ideas even grow on trees – ask Newton!

STEP 1   Commit your top management group

If you are the chief executive, your top management group is the group you work with, those who report to you formally, plus perhaps one or two other senior 'influencers'. If you're not the CEO, then it's the top management group, full stop. A second best is to win commitment for the top group in your division or department or whatever – but that may limit the issues you can work on, and the impact you can achieve.

How? Necessarily, by a meeting. This can be overtly a meeting to introduce an innovation programme, or may be initially somewhat more covert – that is, it could be under the guise of 'strategic planning' or 'new product development', or anything which might lead to innovative activity. (Strategic planning can be very useful here.)

This meeting has three major planned outcomes:

- Commitment – as a group, sharing the innovative intent.
- Priority, or initial, opportunity or problem areas – an agreed list of valuable issues that will provide a vehicle for the early Mindmix activities. (This is expanded as Step 2.)
- Identification of the people who will participate, be part of, the early innovative attempts. (This is expanded as Step 3.)

Clearly there may be other outcomes from this meeting, and later notes on 'considerations' raise some points for you.

STEP 2   Recognise and define your initial opportunity or problem areas

Our assumption in this book is that these are already known to you, and so we have not described the available methods for doing this. But if you're disenchanted with the conventional wisdom, try some divergent thinking. You may surprise yourself.

BANK YOUR IDEAS HERE

Getting ideas is easy. Using some of them requires courage –
and while a good idea can be adapted and adopted, management courage can't be!

How? At the commitment meeting. Environmental scanning, SWOT analysis (Strengths, Weaknesses, Opportunities and Threats), portfolio analysis, and other available and much written about search mechanisms may be used. But do it at the commitment meeting . . . then everyone's committed to the programme and what it will initially address.

STEP 3   Identify relevant people

This must include a 'core' innovative group (or groups) who will later assume a leadership or example role in the innovative programme, and will act as 'front-runners'. It should also include considerations of other less directly affected persons – for example, those who might make up an initial idea-generation group for problem 'X'. The 'core' group will be upper-middle to middle managers, the future idea-evaluators.

How? At the commitment meeting. And don't forget to start communicating with these prepared individuals.

Explain. Give them a copy of this book. Win their enthusiasm if you can. If you can't, bargain for at least some of their time. Mindmix offers them potential solutions to their problems too. You should get enough prepared to try to give you a starting point. In a small organisation, you might have a single group of three, four or five people. In a large national organisation, you might have many groups, each of ten or twelve. Organisation structures, tasks and responsibilities will suggest the appropriate form.

STEP 4   Train the people from Step 3

The objective for the 'core' group is understanding of the overall process, and the building of personal competence in some or all of the areas of:

BANK YOUR IDEAS HERE

Doing what you did well yesterday well today reduces the probability of doing well what you need to do well tomorrow!

- Idea-generation
- Idea-evaluation
- Idea protection/improvement.

Which areas will depend on people's backgrounds and their organisational roles, but as most, if not all, members of these groups will be involved in evaluating ideas, that element is likely to be offered to all.

How? For the 'core' group, use the issues from Step 2, the organisational problems/opportunities, as the vehicles for their training and development in Mindmix skills. These issues become the focal point of the idea-generation activities. And the ideas emerging become the subject of the screening and evaluation methods. Finally, the selected ideas or solutions or projects become the focus of the idea-protection activity. Learning occurs in parallel with problem-solving.

For others (not the 'core' group), training may be much simpler, but should be at least what they need for the confidence to contribute effectively.

STEP 5   Multiply the effort

The organisational need is to have workgroups up and down the hierarchy address opportunities, problems, productivity issues, barriers to change or whatever else they believe is holding them back from doing things as they'd like to – which, for most, is doing things more effectively. The next step is to call for or identify volunteer groups who, following training, will use these methods, especially idea-generation, on problems in the workplace.

Managers in your core group(s) can help in this task of identifying and inviting participation. That core group can also expand the range of issues available for these operational teams or project groups to examine. Some teams will flow directly from the 'core' groups' activities. And of course the team or

BANK YOUR IDEAS HERE

Asking groups to be idea-productive assumes they've the time.
If there is no time to think, then there are no ideas!

project groups will have their own ideas about just what should be looked at! Often, however, the core group may wish to nominate issues for initial examination, with the volunteer operational teams nominating their own issues later, when skills and experience are more widely distributed.

How? Explain to the middle and operational levels the push for innovation. Get the rationale clear, and be certain to include all involved third parties, like unions and staff associations.

If management is going to nominate the initial issues to be addressed, clearly delineate them. If it's a 'free choice' on issues, say so.

Then invite participation in idea groups on a genuinely volunteer basis. Coercion, or the hint of it, will kill it. Whether a small or large number of groups respond at this stage is not the most important thing. Getting started is.

Make it clear whether the idea groups are going to elect their own leader/chairperson, or whether the core groups or others in the structure reserve the right to nominate, or influence, team leader selection.

Address the issue of rewards, and make the policy public. The question of time availability also needs public clarification.

Train as necessary.

STEP 6　Keep track of it

Set up a system of keeping information flowing. You and others will want to know about outcomes. You'll be told of many of them anyway, as you receive requests for approval to put some of the new ideas into practice. This means that your 'idea evaluators' will be busy. It also means that those offering the ideas will be wanting to know of your decisions. The 'yesses' are easy to explain – the 'noes' must be accompanied by understandable explanations or the idea flow will dry up.

How? Generalised hints don't help much here. But knowing the organisation and its constraints and customs makes it not too difficult a task.

BANK YOUR IDEAS HERE

All accepted new ideas lead to change. Managing change is a positive concept. People who worry about managing change may be suffering from *neophobia*!

The major point is to do it with minimal institutional mechanisms. Remember you want ideas and outcomes, not a formal, multi-carbon-copy reporting system. Idea group members can use simple 'diaries' (like a school exercise book!) as a means of keeping track amongst themselves, and these also become stepping-off points for groups reporting progress.

Some organisations use 'idea sponsors' as a way of tracking. This is an individual who can find his or her way through the red tape, and keep a project alive.

STEP 7   Reinforce it

By now, the 'installation' is complete. The process is under way. Keeping it going is now the task, and reinforcement is a primary tool.

How? Answer your own 'How do I?' with some divergent thinking. Do you have a company newsletter? Can you create one? What about regular (regional) meetings where people can be told and involved? A 'scoreboard' for the section? (But watch excessive competition!) Do 'special events' at lunchtime in the canteen provide opportunities?

What you're after is maintaining momentum, having success recognised, and establishing credibility for this approach to innovation.

STEP 8   Extend the process

Find and encourage new idea groups. New groups may want a shortlist of issues to consider, but your original idea groups, now experienced, will probably be wanting to select their own issues or problems or opportunities if they are not already doing so. Confidence will be up, because some earlier successes have demonstrated credibility. Involved managers will be more

BANK YOUR IDEAS HERE

Controlling the direction of stimulated innovative activities in an organisation is a little like fighting the wind. Don't start unless you're prepared to accept as yet unrecognised directions.

trusted, and the idea groups know they can make it work.

How? Return to Step 5, and cycle forward again.

When you are working through these steps in your own organisation there are a number of practical considerations to keep in mind. We have experienced them first-hand, and offer these following comments as further clarification. What you have read to this point has, of course, covered the key desirable inclusions for any deliberate attempt to manage an innovation programme. These additional comments attempt to confront some of the 'do's' and 'don'ts' from the installation viewpoint. They've been learnt the hard way; perhaps some consideration of them as you make your own plans will be helpful. And don't forget; there's room for you to make a note or two on the side. The page opposite is your bank.

But before you begin, refer back to page 69 and to the Mindmix message. You will have noted the importance of attracting 'creative people'. While we don't want necessarily to stress this – *all* people have divergent skills – it is important to realise that you can't get unusual ideas from a group of convergent people performing convergent tasks. Search your organisation. What jobs require a degree of divergence, or impose qualitative demands, or confront open-ended problems? Remember the earlier message: 'horses for courses'. Be sure that positions which offer divergent opportunities are filled by people with divergent potential. Then note their names for use in your idea-generation groups.

Management commitment

Any idea-generation programme or innovation programme attempted without the total commitment of the top management group, *all* of them, is likely to hiccup, have troubles, or even worse, die in infancy. Commitment doesn't mean just support. It doesn't mean just understanding. It doesn't mean non-interference. It means what it says.

BANK YOUR IDEAS HERE

Suspending judgment of novel ideas requires personal effort. It's an active, not a passive, process.

A useful starting point for such a programme is to meet with the top group. Take them away from the day-to-day activities, and debate the value and intents of the programme. This may need more than one meeting. Of course, if you haven't the power to take this step easily, you'll have to devise an innovative strategy to convince them. Lock yourself up with a few friends, and try some of the processes in Chapter 7. You might just surprise yourself.

The purposes of this meeting or meetings is to:

- Gain commitment
- Test understanding
- Plan support
- Clarify roles
- Select initial steps
- Ensure preparedness to invest time, money and support resources.

Innovation programmes can and do work. They can cause ideas to bound around an organisation. They can cause change. They can challenge the existing, institutionalised processes and procedures. They invite people to think, to doubt, to question. If the top management group isn't ready for this, then there's no point in proceeding.

Fear of change is often only a reaction to the unknown. It's human. It's perfectly normal. But an early meeting can erode the edges of the unknown, can put the programme in a clear light and reassure the anxious.

Take a bite-sized beginning

Starting with the entire organisation is probably only desirable if your organisation is relatively small. How small is small? There's no exact figure. Perhaps, if you can't begin without affecting everyone in the organisation, then you're small.

BANK YOUR IDEAS HERE

Living with new ideas and change can be a worry. Living without them must be absolutely depressing!

Of course, if you manage a discrete group, there's no reason why you can't begin using tools and concepts from Chapters 7 and 8 immediately. You are 'the top management'. But if you're in a more complex position, or a more complicated organisation, we suggest selecting a cooperative sub-unit. Perhaps one division? Or perhaps one site, or one department.

Limiting the size of what you begin with doesn't mean taking inconsequential issues. Leave the trivial things for trival methods. Take significant issues, even at the beginning. Try the old chestnuts. Do go for new products or new services.

Take an organisational viewpoint

This may sound contradictory to the previous point, but it's not. What we mean is: in whatever sub-organisation you choose (*or* the one that chooses to try), be alert to the different roles the members of that organisation will play. In particular, be alert to your senior supervisory/middle management levels. They can be bypassed too easily, and alienated if not involved. Reinforce their traditional role of idea-evaluation. Of course, you may wish to do more than this, and involve them in idea-generation. But at the very least, making it possible for them to receive, evaluate, and feedback on innovative programmes can have tremendous *positive* effects on employee relations. In fact, in one instance in a UK company we used such a programme directly to confront a problem of employee relations. As could be expected:

- It provided people with a chance to contribute.
- It improved communications between middle management, supervisors and operators. Ideas flowed up, feedback and requests for more data flowed down. People simply had to talk to each other.
- It provided a base for mutual respect, common objectives and improved communications.

BANK YOUR IDEAS HERE

Mindmix processes cause people to talk. If you want a quiet ship, don't encourage Mindmix!

Set priorities – but be flexible

Don't simply form groups, and then wait for them to tell you what they want to work on. Nothing in any approach to managing innovation should suggest management abdication. Tell people what you consider to be important areas. But remember that once they start these powerful processes, they may recognise other opportunities. They may want some input into your priority setting. (Of course, if such involvement frightens you, don't start at all.)

Train/educate

At all levels. People involved primarily with idea-generation often can't just jump into it. They need to be prepared. And no MBA programme we know of deals with the 'how' of those processes. Take time to brief groups properly, to practise the idea-generation techniques, to review decision-making/idea-evaluation processes in the organisation, to practise the idea-improvement logic. You're not only giving your people confidence, you're investing in their potential. It's *purposeful* training and development, and will almost certainly be very much more productive than conventional classroom-based 'training programmes'.

Don't demand – encourage

No one can be forced to give ideas, and no organisational innovation programme can be imposed by edict. But encouragement is essential. If you want new ideas, do be prepared to live with some very odd thoughts. And respect those oddities; they're probably evidence that attempts at divergent thinking are being made.

BANK YOUR IDEAS HERE

Beware the *neophiliac*. Loving change for change's sake is a
bad base for evaluating the new against the old!

The best encouragement for ideas is simply that a total innovative process is visible. Let people see that ideas are being
received. Let people know what has happened to ideas. Your
company newspaper or staff magazine might provide an adequate extra medium, but the basic channel is the active
involvement of managers and supervisors at all levels. They
can, and should, talk to people about what's happening. And
this channel's always available – encourage it to operate!

Realistic expectations

Too many managers are disappointed at the early output from
their attempts at stimulating innovation. They seem to expect a
new product, or a new programme, suddenly to emerge
complete as if by metamorphosis, and are distressed when all
they see are stumbling attempts at divergence.

Entering into a total innovation programme is no small step.
It can, and usually does, impact on the culture of the organisation. And cultures don't change quickly. Also, remember
you're fighting against a long history of credible convergence.
Desirable divergence may be a reality for you, and for your
people, but you and they are probably out-of-practice, and
operating in an environment where not everyone may want
you to succeed. Keep your early expectations realistic. But do
expect long-term change and long-term gain.

Praise success – don't knock failures

It's very easy to fall into the trap of repeating history, of joining
the 'knockers'. A little self-discipline is required here.

If you've received an apparently stupid idea, return it and ask
'How can we make this work?' This question will either kill the
idea, or determine that it's a valid idea. Or ask for alternative

BANK YOUR IDEAS HERE

Odd thoughts make us uncomfortable. They might also make us successful.

ideas to compare with an isolated idea. Or share your evaluative criteria. But don't just say 'no!', and don't bother to record
failures. Save your energy for recognising the bumble bee that
is flying.

Don't offer bribes

We've seen both incentive-based idea schemes and those without incentives work. But the former tend to be temporary
phenomena. Certainly, incentive-based schemes work – but
why was the incentive necessary? Because ideas weren't
coming forth as a normal part of the day's work. They had to be
made a special case.

Where the climate is idea-assisting, where you've done what
you can to lower the obstacles, where you've started to *ask*,
you'll get ideas. People, particularly working together in
groups, like to contribute.

Of course, not offering bribes doesn't mean you cannot
reward. If a group makes a significant contribution, obviously
some sort of financial rewards may be a good idea if they are
consistent with your organisation's culture and policies. They
are concrete recognitions of contribution. But if they are
impossible, make 'legitimate rewards' the subject of your idea
group's next meeting.

Mix groups carefully

It happens rarely, but occasionally we come across groups
which are made up of individuals either all dominantly quantitative or all dominantly qualitative. Neither are satisfactory.
Don't build up groups of only engineers, or only salespeople, or
only anything. If you haven't got a way of planning a group
(e.g. using DPA), then at least aim for different backgrounds, or
different functions.

BANK YOUR IDEAS HERE

Do something different today/now! Perhaps you will trigger a new thought.

Love 'em, leave 'em – and revisit 'em

Make it clear to groups you form, at any level, that you *care* – you do want to hear what they come up with, irrespective of how odd or how irrelevant it may at first seem.

Leave them to get on with the task. Over-involved managers, particularly senior managers, cause two effects in groups even when they deliberately avoid domination. They act like a wet blanket for many: 'I would have suggested something, but I though I'd better not as Big Ben was there, and he would have thought I was stupid.' Or they act as a stimulus for the 'point-scorer', the individual who has a lot to say when the boss is present. And 'point-scorers' are rarely your divergent resource.

But do call back from time to time. Show your interest is continuing. We've seen good potential idea groups die for want of nothing more than a simple revisit.

Idea sponsors/idea champions

Once ideas start to flow, even those first evaluated as possibilities may need some protection. Look around – somewhere at a senior level is a more-or-less universally trusted individual, who knows the organisation inside-out. Such people make excellent 'sponsors' or 'champions' to keep a watching brief on a new idea, to cut red-tape for the responsible group and to give encouragement as needed.

Mindmix programmes don't *need* sponsors or champions, but they certainly make the process easier. But only if they're trusted both up and down the organisation.

Give resources

What do groups need? Not much. A little time to get started. Somewhere to meet. Perhaps some training help. Perhaps some

BANK YOUR IDEAS HERE

'Participation' is as simple as asking a question. Any question.

machine-shop time to try out an idea before they bring it to you. Perhaps a little market research data (that might already be on file).

Encouragement and support can clearly go beyond simple expressions of good-will. There can be money involved. You're used to measuring return on investment but in innovation programmes the possible returns are not always clear when the modest, initial investment (time or whatever) is called for. But one thing is for sure – nothing ventured, nothing gained! A little internal 'venture capital' may be required. You can't innovate without some risk.

Trust

Groups, like individuals, will 'goof off'. And not all groups will yield constructive new ideas. But people generally are concerned with opportunities to contribute, not just with having fun. Certainly, groups moving into divergence will be having fun, and to the external observer they may appear to be doing anything but work. Don't lose faith at this stage. What's wrong with work being fun? Particularly if that 'having fun' results in a great new idea.

Expect your sacred cows to suffer

You can close down idea-generation easily. One simple way is to put some things 'off limits'. So you've got a pet product, or a favourite programme, or something you introduced ten years ago when you were coming up the organisation. Don't limit your groups by putting such projects in the 'don't touch' category. If you do, you'll simply find you generate a belief that the process is a game. 'We're not really free to come up with ideas. Let's give them what they want and get back to the safety of work.'

BANK YOUR IDEAS HERE

Innovation is no big thing . . . at least, not necessarily. Small ideas can be important.

Your sacred cows may even be the first to be challenged by something new. But objective evaluation should establish whether your sacred cow has been replaced by the new, improved model. It may not be – there's no guarantee that the new ideas will be better than the old. But if they are – what's the trade-in value of outdated sacred cows?

Communicate, communicate – and communicate

Then talk about it a little more. This is critical. Idea schemes which operate like a secret society are more likely to cause your employee relations pains than to provide idea gains. Wooden boxes on walls and closed-door 'Idea Review Committees' have nothing at all to do with the processes discussed in this book. Open communication has a lot to do with Mindmix. People need to know the 'what?', 'why?' and 'how?' of the innovative effort they're being asked to get involved with. They need to know if it's working elsewhere in the organisation, particularly when they're bogged down. They need to know why an idea has been rejected – what criteria were used (they may even see holes in the criteria). They need to know what savings and gains have been made.

Mindmix *is* a communicative process. It depends on open requests for contribution, open acceptance and recognition of contribution, honest feedback of what's happened, etc. These are all just words. It simply depends on people talking openly about what's going on.

One method you might use is a 'diary' system. We use this successfully. It's very simple. Groups keep a diary of what they're doing and have done. They simply make this available to others that are interested (e.g. management).

TEN IDEAS FOR MANAGING CHANGE

1   Accept 'managing change' as a normal responsibility. Innovation intent ought to be part of any manager's role, and change is part and parcel of successful innovation.

2   Look at your own attitude to change: are you a neophobiac (one who fears change) or a neophiliac (one who loves change)? Acknowledge the impact of this on those who work with you. If you're out of synchronisation with your work team, clearly issues of change can become sources of conflict.

3   View change as a necessary element of the innovative process. Be sure of which part of this process you're in, and communicate this to your people.

4   Encourage participation. Most resistance to change flows from ignorance and non-involvement.

5   View changes as job-affecting, rather than as people-affecting. Of course change affects people, but it often does so by changing what they do (their jobs). Look at the jobs; you can take action to redesign jobs, but redesigning people is clearly not as easy.

6   To introduce a major change, break it up into manageable components, *but* introduce each component (change) quickly. Extending the introduction of a change can lengthen the period of people's discomfort!

7   Use projected cause-effect probabilities to draw up contingent plans when introducing a change, and stay flexible to initiate them. Include plans for probable people problems.

8   Use training to raise consciousness of desirable change. Provide people with tools to aid generation of desirable changes, and to properly plan implementation.

9   Don't generalise about 'resistance to change'. It can too easily be a 'cop-out' for not properly managing the predictable effects of a change.

10 Accept that for organisation development (i.e. purposeful long-term change) to occur smoothly, it goes hand-in-hand with management development.

Be prepared to measure

Investing in a total innovative effort may not cost you a lot but, as we said before, it may need some committed resources. And such programmes are risky; there's no guarantee of a payback.

Now, you wouldn't get involved in a risk investment of any other type without measuring your return at fixed intervals. Total innovation programmes are no different. The diary concept mentioned earlier should be useful here. The system we use keeps a record of gain or savings per group and per idea. And as it is readily available, it provides a simple check on return.

You should be now ready to try to implement a Mindmix programme in your own organisation. How easy it is for you to begin will depend on many things, not least of which is your position. But if you review the key **action** chapters, you should be able to start some degree of innovation effort. We consider these chapters to be:

- **Chapter 7:** Creative tools for groups (Many Involved Xpressly). Which group processes can you try? With whom?
- **Chapter 8:** Handling ideas once you've got them (Maximising Integrative Xchanges). How are your decision-making/idea-evaluation processes and your surveying of future processes: healthy? What can you do to improve them, to build teams for effective Mindmix?
- **Chapter 9:** How to get started in your organisation (Mindmix In Xecution). You've just worked through this Mix, and may have made some useful practical and personal notes.

Good luck in your attempts. There's no doubt that innovation is the pathway to business excellence, and that effective management of it is the pathway to organisational excellence. May you find the pathway without too many detours, and may you find it paved with new opportunities.

REFERENCES

Chapter 2   Your two brains

1   Mintzberg, H., 'Planning on the Left Side and Managing on the Right', *Harvard Business Review*, July–August 1976.
2   Crane, L., in *Creativity Network*, Vol. 7, No. 3, Nov. 1981, (pp. 27–28).
3   Interview by Elizabeth Shey Gorovitz, 'The Creative Brain II: A Revisit with Ned Hermann' in *Training & Development Journal*, December 1982, (pp. 74–88).
4   Torrance, E. P., Reynolds, C., Bull, D. E. & Riczel, T., '*Revised (1978) Norms – Technical Manual for Your Style of Learning & Thinking*', (for availability direct enquiries to Paul Torrance, Georgia Studies of Creative Behaviour, Dept of Educational Psychology, University of Georgia, Athens, Georgia, USA).
5   Schwartz, S. A., and De Mattei, R., 'Mobius Psi-Q Test', *Omni Magazine* (October, 1981). The questions appear in William Taggart and E. Paul Torrance, *Human Information Processing*™ *Survey* (Bensenville, Illinois: Scholastic Testing Service, Inc. 1983).
6   Kable, J. C., Hicks, R. E., & Smith, N.I., *DPA: The Users' Guide*, Sydney, NIS, 1984. Also Kable, J. C., *People, Preferences & Performance*, Jacaranda-Wiley, 1988. (For availability, enquiries to NIS Associates, Sydney, Australia).

Chapter 3   The manager and innovation

1   Torrance, E. P., *Education & the Creative Potential*, University of Minnesota, 1963, p. 21.
2   Quarton, G. C, 'Deliberate Efforts to Control Human Behaviour and Modify Personality', *Daedalus, Journal of the American Academy of Arts and Sciences*, No. 3, 1967.

Chapter 5   Innovation and strategic planning

1   Herbert, F., *Whipping Star*, G. P. Putnam's Sons, 1969.
2   Turner, G., 'ICI becomes proactive', *Long Range Planning*, Vol. 17, No. 6, 1984, pp. 12, 13.
3   'The new breed of strategic planner', *Business Week*, 17 September 1984.
4   Adapted from *Strategic Planning Structures*, NIS Associates, Sydney, 1988.

Chapter 6   Creative tools for the individual

1   Clarke, C. H., & Smith, N. I., *Idea Management*, NIS Associates, 1982.
2   Rickards, T., *Problem Solving Through Creative Analysis*, Gower Press, 1974.
3   Osborn, A., *Applied Imagination*, Charles Scribner, 1953.

Chapter 7   Creative tools for groups

1   Clarke, C. H., & Smith, N.I., *Idea Management*, NIS Associates, 1982.

Chapter 8   Handling ideas once you've got them

1   *MINDMIX* Training Materials*, NIS Associaties, 1987.
2   Developed by Stevens, B., Manchester Business School, United Kingdom.

FURTHER READING

This list is in sections, clearly headed. If you have a particular interest in one or more areas, you should be able to find suitable reading here. Listed items include both books and articles.

Organisational and managerial view of innovation

These are general texts in the area for the most part offering an organisational rather than an individual or small group perspective.

Blake, R. S., & Mouton, J. S., *Productivity & Creativity: a Social Dynamics Approach*, American Management Association, 1981.

de Bono, E., *Opportunities*, Penguin Books, 1980.

Jones, B., *Sleepers, Wake! Technology & the Future of Work*, Oxford University Press, 1982.

Kable, J. C., Hicks, R. E., & Smith, N. I., *DPA: The Users' Guide*, NIS Associates, 1984.

Kanter, R. M., 'The Middle Manager as Innovator', *Harvard Business Review*, July–August 1982.

Kanter, R. M., *The Change Masters, Corporate Entrepreneurs at Work*, Unwin, 1983.

Nystrom, H., *Creativity & Innovation*, Wiley 1979.

Ohmae, K., *The Mind of the Strategist*, Penguin Books, 1983.

Peters, T. J., & Waterman, R. H., *In Search of Excellence*, Harper & Row 1983.

Pinchot, Gifford, *Intrapreneuring, or Why You Don't Have to Leave the Corporation to Become an Entrepreneur*, Harper & Row, 1984.

Ramo, S., *The Management of Innovative Technological Corporations*, Wiley Interscience, 1980.

Reitz, H. J., *Behaviour in Organisations* (chapter 'Creativity & Innovation'), Irwin, 1981.

Rickards, T., *Stimulating Innovation*, Frances Pinter, 1985.

Roberts, E. B., 'Generating Effective Corporate Innovation,' *Technology Review*, Oct./Nov. 1977.

Smith, N. I., 'Creativity & Organisational Innovation', *Human Resource Management Australia*, Vol. 18, No. 2, 1980 (August).

Smith, N. I., & Ainsworth, M., *Ideas Unlimited: The Mindmix approach to innovative management*, Nelson 1985.

Stoner, J. A. F., Yetton, P. W., & Collins, R. R., *Management in Australia*, Prentice-Hall, 1985.

Tushman, M. L., & Moore, W. L., *Readings in the Management of Innovation*, Pitman, 1982.

Twiss, B., *Managing Technological Innovation*, Longman, 1980.

Whitfield, P. R., *Creativity in Industry*, Penguin Books 1975.

Zaltman, G., Duncan, R., & Holbeck, J., *Innovations & Organisations*, Wiley, 1973.

The 'rational' management processes

These publications may be useful to you should you wish to pursue processes mentioned in Chapters 4, 5 and 8. They describe essentially convergent, analytical approaches.

Ansoff, H. I., *Corporate Strategy*, Penguin Books, 1977.

Argenti, J., *Practical Corporate Planning*, Allen & Unwin, 1980.

Dean, B. V. (ed.), *Project Management: Methods & Studies*, Elsevier, 1985.

Drucker, P. F., *Managing for Results*, Pan Books, 1964.

Humble, J. W., *Management by Objectives*, Gower Press, 1972.

Kepner, C., & Tregoe, B., *The Rational Manager*, McGraw Hill, 1965.

Lipton, H. A., & Turoff, M., *The Delphi Method: Techniques and Application*, Addison-Wesley, 1975.

Mason, R., & Mitroff, J., *Challenging Strategic Planning Assumptions: Theory, Case and Techniques*, Wiley, 1981.

Odiorne, G. S., *MBO II*, Fearon Pitman, 1979.

Ohmae, K., *The Mind of the Strategist*, Penguin Books, 1983.

Sprouster, J., *TQC: Total Quality Control*, Horwitz Grahame, 1984.

Stallworthy, E. A., & Kharbanda, O. P., *Total Project Management*, Gower, 1983.

Left brain, right brain

Those who wish to pursue Chapter 2 can do so from the following list. However, be on the look-out for a new titles; the area is fast-moving, and this is not intended to be a comprehensive bibliography.

Agor, W. H., *Intuitive Management: Integrating Left and Right Brain Management Skills*, Prentice Hall, 1984.

Agor, W. H., 'Brain Skill Development in Management Training', *Training & Development Journal*, April 1983.

Gowan, J. C., 'The Production of Creativity Through Right Hemisphere Imagery', *Journal of Creative Behaviour*, Vol. 13, No. 1, 1979.

Kable, J. C., 'Decision Preference Analysis – Measuring a Manager's Preference for Managing', *Journal of Management Development*, Vol. 2, No. 3, 1983.

Kable, J., *People, Preferences and Performance*, John Wiley, 1988.

Koestler, A., *The Act of Creation*, Macmillan, 1964.

McCallum, R. S., & Glynn, S. M., 'Hemispheric Specialisation and Creative Behaviour', *Journal of Creative Behaviour*, Vol 13, No. 4, 1979.

Mintzberg, H., 'Planning on the left side and managing on the right', *Harvard Business Review*, July–Aug. 1976.

Myers, J. T., 'Hemisphericity Research: An Overview with Some Implications for Problem Solving', *Journal of Creative Behaviour*, Vol. 16, No. 3, 1982.

Russell, P., *The Brain Book*, Routledge & Kegan Paul, 1979.

Sperry, R. W., 'Lateral Specialisation of Cerebral Function in the Surgically Separated Hemispheres', in McGuigan, F. J., & Schoonover, R. A., *The Psychophysiology of Thinking*, Academic Press, 1973.

Springer, S. P. & Deutsch, G., *Left Brain, Right Brain*, W. H. Freeman, 1981.

Creative thinking, idea generation and creativity in general

These are general works in the area of creativity which the very interested reader may wish to pursue. Some are classics in the field, albeit a little dated.

Adams, J. L., *Conceptual Blockbusting – A Guide to Better Ideas*, Norton & Co., 1980.

Albrecht, K., *Brain Power: Learn to Improve your Thinking Skills*, Prentice Hall, 1980.

Buzan, T., *Make the Most of Your Mind*, Pan Books, 1977.

Clark, C. H., *The Crawford Slip-Writing Method*, Yankee Ingenuity Programmes, 1978.

Creativity & Innovation Network. This quarterly journal published by the Manchester Business School, UK, contains a variety of papers in this general subject area.

de Bono, E., *Lateral Thinking for Management*, McGraw-Hill (undated).

de Bono, E., *Opportunities*, Penguin Books, 1980.

de Bono, E., *Practical Thinking*, Penguin Books, 1976.

Davis, G. A., *Creativity is Forever*, Badger Press, 1981.

Gilchrist, M. B., 'The Definition & Identification of Creativity', *Human Resource Management Australia*, Summer 1979–80.

Gordon, W. J. J., *Synectics: The Development of Creative Capacity*, Harper & Row, 1961.

Hayes, J. R., *The Complete Problem Solver*, Franklin Institute Press, 1981.

Jones, M., *Getting High on Creativity*, Rosen Press, 1982.

Jones, S., & Sims, D., 'Mapping as an Aid to Creativity', *Journal of Management Development*, Vol. 4, No. 1, 1985.

Litvak, S., *Use Your Head: how to develop the other 80% of your brain*, Prentice-Hall, 1982.

Lynch, D., *Your High Performance Business Brain*, Prentice Hall, 1984.

Miller, W. C., *The Creative Edge*, Addison-Wesley, 1987.

Nayak, P. R., & Ketteringham, J., *Breakthroughs!*, Mercury Books (W.H. Allen), 1987.

Osborn, A. F., *Applied Imagination*, Scribner, 1952.

Parnes, S. J., Noller, R. B., & Biondi, A. M., *Guide to Creative Action*, Scribner, 1977.

Prince, G., *The Practice of Creativity*, Harper & Row, 1970.

Rickards, T., *Problem Solving through Creative Analysis*, Gower Press, 1974.

Rickards, T., *Creativity At Work*, Gower Press, 1988.

Savary, L. M., & Ehlen-Miller, M., *Mindways: A guide for Exploring Your Mind*, Harper & Row, 1979.

Schlicksupp, H., 'Idea Generation for Industrial Firms,' *R & D Management*, Vol. 1, No. 2, 1977.

Smith, M., Beck, Cooper, Cox, Ottaway & Talbot, *Introducing Organisational Behaviour*, Macmillan, 1982.

Steiner, G. A. (ed.), *The Creative Organisation*, University of Chicago Press, 1965.

Suojanen, W. W., 'Creativity, Management and the Minds of Man', *Human Resource Management Australia*, Winter 1980.

Torrance, E. Paul, *The Search for Satori & Creativity*, Creative Education Foundation, 1979.

Van Gundy, A. B., *Training Your Creative Mind*, Prentice-Hall, 1982.

Von Oech, R., *A Whack on the Side of the Head – How to Unlock your mind for Innovation*, Warner Books, 1983.

Testing creativity

This is an area of limited and difficult research. The experts are far from agreed, and over the years interest has varied. If you are interested, these are some general sources which provide a basic reference to the range of tests available. These include the following:

A bibliography of various measures in:

Kaltsounis, B., 'Instruments Useful in Studying Creative Behaviour & Creative Talent', *Journal of Creative Behaviour*, Vol. 5, 2nd qtr 1971, pp. 117–26, and Davis, G. A., *ditto*, Vol. 5, 3rd qtr 1971, pp 162–5.

A description of measures of divergent thinking in:

Gilchrist, M., *The Psychology of Creativity*, Melbourne University Press, 1972 (pp. 19–23).

In addition, you may wish to refer to the following:

Guildford, J. P., 'Creativity', *American Psychologist*, Vol. 5, 1950.
Kable, J. C., Hicks, R. E., & Smith, N.I., *DPA: the User's Guide*, NIS Associates, 1984.
Torrance, E. P., Reynolds, C., Bell, O. E., & Riegel, T., '*Revised (1978) norms-technical manual for Your Style of Learning & Thinking*'. Enquiries to Paul Torrance, Georgia Studies of Creative Behaviour, Dept of Educational Psychology, University of Georgia, Athens, Georgia, USA.

A general reference to tests of all kinds (not just of creativity), and one much used by professionals in the area is:

Buros, O. K., *The Mental Measurements Yearbook*, Gryphon Press.

An index to this major reference work is in:

Buros, O. K. (ed.), *Personality Tests & Reviews*, Gryphon Press, 1970.
Also by Buros *Tests in Print: A comprehensive bibliography*, Gryphon Press, 1961, *Tests in Print II: an index to Tests, test reviews, etc.*, Gryphon Press, 1974.

Innovation and research and development groups

This is not a distinctly different topic; even R & D group processes start with an idea – and R & D management is still management. However, there are special considerations (e.g. resources) in R & D work, and these publications are specific to this area.

Frohman, A. L., 'The Performance of Innovation: Managerial Roles', *California Management Review*, Vol. 20, No. 3, 1978.
Gibson, J. E., *Managing Research & Development*, Wiley, 1981.
Glassman, E., 'Managing for Creativity: back to basics in R & D', *R & D Management*, 1986, Vol. 16, No. 2.
Kay, N. M., *The Innovating Firm; A behavioural theory of Corporate R & D*, Macmillan, 1979.

Pelz, D. C., & Andrews, F. M., *Scientists in Organisations – Productive Climates for Research and Development*, Wiley, 1966.

Ramo, S., *The Management of Innovative Technological Corporations*, Wiley-Interscience, 1980.

Twiss, B., *Managing Technological Innovation*, Longman, 1980.

Whitfield, P. R., *Creativity in Industry*, Penguin, 1975.

Product development

These publications may provide a broader frame of reference if you are heavily involved in new product development. Some offer comments on matrix approaches which are more specific than those raised in Chapter 7. However, the open-ended formats in Chapter 7 may encourage more divergent thinking.

Andrews, B., *Creative Product Development*, Longman, 1975.

Carson, J. W., & Rickards, T., *Industrial New Product Development – A Manual; for the 1980's*, Gower Press, 1979.

Crawford, C. M., *New Product Management*, Irwin, 1987.

von Hippel, E. A., 'Users as Innovators', *Technology Review*, Jan. 1978.

Mathot, G. B. M., 'How to Get New Products to Market Quicker', *Long Range Planning*, Vol. 15, No. 6, 1982.

Midgley, D. F., *Innovation & New Product Marketing*, Croom Helm, 1977.

Takeuchi, H., & Nonaka, I. 'The New Product Development Game', *Harvard Business Review*, Jan.–Feb. 1986.

Twiss, B., *Managing Technological Innovation*, Longman, 1980.

We hope you have enjoyed this book.

If you have any thoughts, concerns or successes you would like to talk through, we would be pleased to hear from you.

NS
MA

NIS Associates
PO Box 124
Manly
Sydney, NSW, 2095
Australia

Any inquiries about the DPA should also be forwarded to the above address.

INDEX